Bespoke.

How to radically grow your bar and restaurant business through **personalisation**

KAMILA LAURA SITWELL

R∃THINK PRESS

First published in Great Britain 2018
by Rethink Press (www.rethinkpress.com)

Contents

Introduction

'You have your way. I have my way. As for the right way,
the correct way, and the only way, it does not exist.'
—Friedrich Nietzsche

Picture the scene: it's 6.30pm, early March, a side street in London's trendy East End, less than a mile from the City, and it's been dark for the best part of an hour. An unforgiving wind drives sleet towards the glistening pavements and whips up the afternoon's soft snow, so it dances in furious circles. Pedestrians keep their heads down, trying to run across the ice as well as they can. Scared they might unceremoniously hit the deck, they shriek in mock terror, then laugh. The buses are crammed with commuters, weary and grateful to have found shelter, trying to catch a glimpse of their stop through the streaks of condensation. The heavy sky has an eerie orange glow and threatens to dump another frozen load before the night is over.

It's Monday – not a great start to the working week – and not an evening you would choose for lingering outside. But Dan and his girlfriend Zoë are out in the cold, shivering and stamping their feet to keep warm. They huddle together halfway down a queue at a discreet doorway, with at least ten people ahead of them and the same number behind. People of all ages, from Millennials to Baby Boomers, and even a couple who must be in their seventies, huddle closely together. Despite their chattering teeth, the people in the queue are lively and sociable. No one seems to care about the bitter cold.

A young woman wearing a black puffer jacket is stationed at the entrance. She responds to her Bluetooth headset and a party of four is ushered forward through the doors, disappearing from view. A buzz of excitement ripples through the queue – not long to go now, for sure.

Zoë shows Dan the selfie of them both she's just posted on Instagram. They laugh and he immediately likes and shares it. Their ice-cold thumbs have no trouble updating their social media accounts, and almost as soon as they post, their friends respond. Everyone in their contact list now knows what Dan's surprise for Zoë's twenty-eighth birthday is – dinner at one of the most sought-after restaurants in London. One that doesn't take reservations but has a reputation that makes it worth queuing for, no matter what the weather is like.

Up and down the country, restaurants and bars are attracting crowds of guests, eager for an experience beyond a standard two-course set menu or a pint of mass-produced lager. This trend made me curious to discover the secret to their success in an industry which is even seeing large chains go to the wall.

The answer is that they have a bespoke offering, and this is what I believe the future of hospitality looks like. And I want to share my insights with you into how you can achieve this.

My story

Since I arrived in the UK as a Polish immigrant over twenty years ago, I have amassed a vast amount of experience in the hospitality industry and corporate world. I wanted to study, work hard and make a better life for myself, but arriving in a foreign country with very little in the bank, I had to start at the bottom. I needed to pay my tuition fees and bills, so I worked for various establishments as a kitchen porter, gradually rising to manage pubs and bars. I absolutely loved working in these environments, not just because of the rich variety of people I met along the way, but also because they taught me some valuable life skills, such as:

- Multitasking – there's no such thing as 'one thing at a time' in a bar. In this industry, I learnt how to do a lot of things at the same time, and how to do them well

- Communication – working as a server is good practice for a career in sales. Day in, day out, my job was to push a product by communicating effectively and building rapport with customers

- Resilience – front-of-house staff tend to be first in the line of fire when customers get angry, and drawing on my resilience helped me bounce back from criticisms and complaints

- Patience – it's called 'waiting' on tables for a reason. Hospitality demands courtesy, so no bullying customers into choosing a starter or rushing them out the door at the end of an evening. Customisation and dealing with hesitation and indecision are all part of the serving experience

- Attention to detail – learning to focus on accuracy is key in this sector. Making sure that everything is prepared and presented correctly

- Sales equals profit; profit equals happy boss. Effectively up-selling and managing guest expectations means more tips

But what fascinates me most about the hospitality industry are the miracles and dramas I witness every day. Bars and restaurants are special places for creating relationships, communities and social gatherings. Away from home and away from work, anything can happen – and often does! I've seen people falling madly in love at first sight, and I've seen long-married couples having nothing to talk about throughout the whole meal, all the love and affection they once felt for each other gone. I've been moved to tears by romantic marriage proposals, and when long-lost families or friends reunite. I've eavesdropped on groups of friends betraying each other with gossip, while at another table a great business deal is being sealed.

There's no other industry like hospitality. You can witness the whole panoply of life taking place right in front of you. In this respect, hospitality is the most fascinating and magical industry of all.

After ten years in the front line, I'd put myself through university. With a degree in business and an MBA in marketing, combined with post-grad qualifications in finance and management, I was ready to take the leap into the corporate world. I had dreams of landing a glamorous job in London, enjoying all the benefits that go with steady employment. The reality is that a job offering hard work, long hours, minimum wage, and limited or no training or opportunities isn't ever going to attract young people looking for long-term career growth. I was ready for a new direction in my life.

However, even then, the jobs I chose were usually connected to hospitality, be it the world of coffee, spirits or soft drinks. This time, though, my involvement came through data, science and analytics focusing on the out-of-home market.

Every marketing graduate I knew at the time aspired to be involved in branding. They were eager to express their creativity and imprint their DNA in brand creation, communicating their vision through powerful marketing campaigns. But this was not for me. Instead, I thrived on working with data and analytics. Admittedly, this was neither sexy nor glamorous, but it was the perfect place for me.

In charge of market and consumer intelligence, I spent my time scouring data, all the while gaining insights into understanding the forecasts from leading global research agencies. I learnt about every aspect of the hospitality industry from a more systematic direction by investigating trends, market dynamics, brand and menu performance, and the reasons behind consumers' changing behaviour. My work day was filled with data, data and more data as I looked for patterns in the mountain of stats and charts, de-coding seemingly unrelated information – a headache for most, but not for a left-brain thinker like me.

To back up the wealth of knowledge I was gaining, I visited pubs, bars and restaurants at every opportunity. I observed guests, analysed their behaviour, and conducted hundreds of interviews with bar and restaurant managers, mixologists, baristas, floor staff, chefs and servers – practically anyone who could contribute to my understanding of the industry.

Knowledge is power. Having access to global insights and industry expertise is invaluable to anyone who can connect the dots and bring the knowledge they gain back to their brand in a credible and relevant way. However, dedicating the time and resources to examining every aspect of the world of hospitality and foodservice is not something many operators can afford while they're running their businesses. But if they find the time and resources, the rewards are priceless.

My interest in this side of the business knows no bounds, and I soon began writing blogs under the heading of 'Divine Eating Out'. Based on my research, I covered new trends in cocktails, garnishes, menus, Millennial-guests' requirements, the female customer and their expectations, the requirements of families, and all sorts of new ways of socialising out of home. As a result, I gained thousands of followers and networked with leading bar and restaurant brands as both my knowledge and authority increased.

Yet I was feeling frustrated by not being able to do much with the bank of valuable information to which I was privy, beyond advising on a new drink concept or sector-specific threats or opportunities. I felt incredibly inspired by insights from the smartest and most passionate people in the industry and the leading data research agencies – I was always told 'Without data, you're just another person with an opinion'. But now it dawned on me that if business leaders had no valid opinion, then they were just people with data. Quite frankly, what's the point in that?

My passion for understanding what my research was telling me grew. After so many years in the industry, I found I could instinctively connect the dots and extract the true meaning of each insight. Having worked in the sector and witnessed many of the trends first hand, I had now backed my insights up with stats. I constantly experienced 'Aha, so this is why so and so happened' moments. It was all making new sense to me.

For example, at one time, I had no idea that a 'wet-led' pub was a tried and tested format, selling cheap mainstream beer mainly to old men, with massive closure rates. However, this offer was simply no longer appealing to guests. In hindsight, it saddened me that I didn't understand the changing trends back then, because perhaps I could have saved certain pubs from inevitable closure. I can still see landlords pulling their hair out in despair as their pubs rapidly lost money.

When consumers are fed up with mediocracy and yearning for something more special and sophisticated, it's an opportunity to pivot. Hindsight is definitely a powerful thing, but knowledge is even more powerful, especially for those who can connect the dots first and win the biggest prize.

College friends Julian Metcalfe and Sinclair Beecham were sick of processed food and boring sandwiches. One thing that caught their attention was how a certain supermarket had introduced a new pre-packed sandwich concept with fresh, tasty combinations. Metcalfe and Beecham studied the model carefully and set about adapting this idea in a bid to revolutionise the British take-out sandwich industry, but in a more accessible format. However, the first investors they approached just laughed – they didn't believe anyone would be remotely interested in sandwiches! They only stopped laughing when Metcalfe and Beecham's Pret a Manger concept captured Britons' imagination and lured them in with fresh and exciting ready-to-go food. Last time I checked, the chain was worth £1.5bn. Not bad for such a 'boring' concept.

Timing in business is everything. My ongoing passion for hospitality, together with the analytical skills and knowledge I've acquired, has revealed to me why the UK hospitality industry is in such turmoil right now. It is going through a sustained period of dynamic change with significant challenges, but also opportunities.

In 2018, the UK eating and drinking out industry was worth £87.9bn, representing a growth of nearly 2% on the previous year, according to MCA Insights. Eating out is becoming a habitual activity – a quick breakfast here, coffee on the go there, sushi before catching the train home, a catch up with colleagues after work, or a spontaneous family lunch after the kids' football game.

There are now 326,000 outlets in the UK, all fiercely competing with each other for consumers.

If you believe your restaurant is in a safe zone because your guests enjoy your food and don't complain, think again. If your guests are not raving in delight because you have exceeded their expectations and their interactions with your brand are always stellar, then nine times out of ten they won't complain, but they will take their business elsewhere. These days, they're spoilt for choices with fancy new restaurants opening up all the time. Although the frequency that consumers were eating out declined (-8%) in 2018, they spent more (+3%) per head, treating themselves to better quality food and drinks.

It's time to wake up to the fact that the rules have changed, because the consumers have changed, so it's never been more important to keep them loyal and encourage repeat business. Ironically, the reasons for consumers' visits to pubs and restaurants are rarely just about food. Today, consumers are in control and a 'one-size-fits-all' approach is history.

Welcome to the experience economy. Bespoke is the future of hospitality, so restaurants and bars need to adapt and build guest-centric businesses. It's time to embrace the movement.

About this book

I've written this book because I'm passionate about the survival of the hospitality industry in all its forms. I understand the whats and the whys of current developments in the industry, and I know how to capitalise on these trends to grow your business to your guests' complete satisfaction. I want each and every part of the sector, from the small family business to the premium offering, to have the right tools, knowledge and guidance at its fingertips.

This book will provide hospitality operators with:

- Help to discover ways to differentiate themselves in the sea of sameness so that they stand out from the competition and attract customers

- Tips and guidance on how to invest appropriately in line with the evolving needs and expectations of guests

- Knowledge based on my years of data analysis and experience within the hospitality industry

- Incisive commentary from leading hospitality insiders who have themselves gained a profound understanding of modern consumers

- Revealing insights to steer a course to customer satisfaction and business success

In Part One, I will outline how customers' needs and habits have changed, from accepting what they were traditionally offered as standard to valuing individual and bespoke experiences above all else. Drawing on a wide body of research and insights from working in the industry, I'll explain why the experience economy is relevant for all aspects of your business, not just branding or food and drink offerings. I'll map out the customer journey, indicating the many touchpoints where your business can make a difference.

In Part Two, I'll discuss how customisation (the central idea of this book) emerges from the deep-seated human desire to choose. I'll discuss the practical applications of customisation and provide you with tips on how to transform your business (or create a new one) with customisation at its heart, illustrating my advice with inspirational case studies and drawing upon expert opinions from leading professionals. My intention is to stimulate your own ideas and prompt you to ask the right questions to discover how to execute a tailored approach as you consider developing your services.

By the time you reach the end of the book, I hope you'll have the tools you need to create, improve, or redesign your own offering to make it appealing for today's guests, thereby ensuring your business's long-term health. I hope I'll have persuaded you to think about not only the food you serve, but also the experience – the connected journey that takes your guests through an exciting process of discovery, highlighting everything that makes modern British hospitality great.

Part One

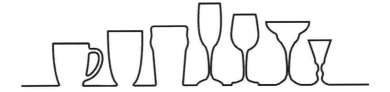

CHAPTER ONE

The Experience Economy

'Food is one part of the experience... But the rest counts as well:
the mood, the atmosphere, the music, the feeling, the design,
the harmony between what you have on the plate and what
surrounds the plate.'
—Alain Ducasse, Michelin Star chef, The Dorchester

In our rapidly changing world, driven as it is by on-the-go technology and instant social media updates, there's one demographic that stands out from the crowd and has every business owner talking – 'Millennials' (born between 1982 and 1999). It's as if this group suddenly appeared from nowhere and now they're the tail wagging the dog.

What's apparent, however, is that while the Millennials are helping to shape market trends, they do not own the market. Their power lies more in their influence on other generations, who are finding that their fresh, original take on life – the way in which they interact with the world – is appealing and accessible. The Millennials are leading the trends, and the older generations, who have more disposable income, are following, and are changing their purchasing behaviours as a result.

Today, over forty-fives are the group most likely to want to customise their meals (45% vs 40% of sixteen to forty-four-year-olds). Mintel Trends helps us to understand changes in the market, so we can target consumers more effectively, and the 'Make it Mine' trend, which is about people's growing desire for a more personalised offer, demonstrates this consumer appreciation for flexibility.

Our eyes have been opened; our taste for new experiences and adventures has been re-awakened. There seems to be no area where the influence of the Millennials hasn't been felt, including casual dining. And businesses need to sit up and take notice of the fact that their more traditional customers have shifted their behaviours and expectations thanks to the influence of the Millennials. Make no mistake, the 'grey pound' still retains its purchasing power, but if your business isn't responding to how these customers are adopting new tastes and habits, then I'm afraid I have news for you: get ready to retire – soon.

With Starbucks apparently able to serve coffee in up to 87,000 different combinations according to what their customers want, now is the time to wake up and (literally) smell the coffee. It's not just technology that's changing fast, it's your customer base. Of course, all demographics matter and there's always room for variety, but to safeguard your business's longevity, you must capture the imagination of the Millennials because they are re-defining all industries. The experience economy has landed on your plate, and it's a main course you can't afford to leave off your menu.

Millennials, Generation Xers and Baby Boomers have far more in common than you may think. Each generation demonstrates that they are increasingly united in common causes, from environmental concerns to humanitarian and animal welfare, to name but a few. One generation draws upon another for knowledge and expertise, and where one leads, another will follow.

When it comes to eating and drinking, 'experiential' and 'multi-sensorial' are fast becoming the standards that most people expect. Understanding these preferences and expectations will help you grow the experience economy your guests demand.

Britain's evolving tastes

Prior to the late 1980s, if you wanted to dine out in most towns and cities, the choices were strictly limited to a local bistro or restaurant, where the waiting staff were more than ready to tell you what you couldn't have, as opposed to what you could have. Any deviation from the menu would frequently be met with complete indifference. Post-war Britain seemed only too ready to celebrate peace without complaint, and without too much choice, either.

As Italian, Indian and Chinese restaurants entered the market, the Britons' enthusiasm to try spicy foreign foods began to grow. By the late 1980s, when the growth in casual dining widened the number of outlets for the masses, people were happy to eat out more often and try new things. It was a boom time for pizza Margaritas and beef lasagnes in shiny new restaurants, or chicken Kievs in the expanding pub-cum-restaurant sector. Dedicated family dining areas, complete with kids' playpens and possibly a clown if you were (un)lucky, encouraged families to dine out together more often. The choices seemed limitless and the casual dining trend took off more quickly than Concorde, at a time when the addition of a fifth terrestrial TV channel made news headlines and topless models winked at tabloid readers from page 3.

At this time, the UK also saw a rise in the chain-store restaurant, with newly created high-street brands focusing on pizzas, pasta and burgers. No matter which outlet you chose, anywhere in the country, the food and level of service were always the same. This was once considered to be a huge selling point, since it reassured the customer. They would know exactly what to expect, and for many, this was what they wanted – reasonably affordable food without too much variation. Nothing wrong with this – Britain deserved to treat itself and feel better after years of post-war hardship, industrial strife, and its forever unpredictable weather.

By the time Britain reached the 1990s, it was ready to put the 'eat' back into 'Great' and armed itself with potato skins loaded with sour cream and chives, topped off with bacon bits. The war on eating at home was in full swing and the restaurant chains were laughing all the way to the bank. Everyone was a winner, customers included. Factory and large-scale battery farming, the widespread use of pesticides, the predisposition to use non-biodegradable packaging, the import of foods at any carbon cost and other environmental issues hadn't entered the collective consciousness, so there was nothing to worry about, was there?

The new consumers

Fast forward thirty years and it's a very different story. This once-winning formula simply doesn't appeal to consumers any more, and it's up to us to understand why people are choosing not to eat in either the big chains or the traditional small outlets as often as they used to. We need to respond to the change in the market and do whatever we can to keep the eating and drinking industry vibrant, relevant and alive.

One of the biggest changes I see is consumers' rejection of the mass-market principle. Perhaps we don't recognise the traditional customer any more because they have changed. They are firmly individual, they want their unique requirements to be catered for, and as a result, they've accidentally invented a marketing term that has reverberated across all demographics – 'decentralised thinking'. This has heads of marketing in all business sectors rushing to conferences and trade talks in order to understand what it means in terms of selling to the new consumer – one who will kick anything that stinks of a homogenous approach into the gutter.

Traditional corporates believed that whatever they put out into the public domain in terms of products, services or information would be accepted as a social norm. That level of complacency nowadays would see them heading for one-star reviews, and God forbid they go viral. The modern-day access to instantaneous information has uncovered the perceived marketing dishonesty of the world we grew up in. Consumers now are more media savvy than previous generations, and their bullshit radars are forever switched on. They scan and deconstruct information fed to them by the mainstream press, the media, governing authorities and big corporations. As a result, they are less open to being manipulated into making purchases. They recognise that manipulation is not about caring for the individual or the environment or society. The term 'mass market' doesn't fit with their need to feel uniquely cared for.

This forms the basis of decentralised thinking.

Modern consumers can spot manipulation and dishonesty at 100 metres and will punish brands if they attempt to pull the wool over their eyes. If they feel they've been fooled once, a brand's customers will shame it. Do it a second time, and the brand will be forever talking to the customers' hands. It's no surprise, therefore, that well-informed consumers attach significance to values, authenticity and honest communication.

The question is, how should brands engage with this trend in meaningful ways? The hospitality sector needs to wake up as quickly as possible, because the old ways of serving customers will soon look like the cold leftovers from a traditional meat and two veg roast.

To help you on your way, I've identified the six top requirements your customers across all generations are likely to look for.

Be unique

'Modern consumers are "food pleasure seekers", adventurous and passionate diners looking for premium experiences at every occasion. The thrill of the experiential has now massively overtaken the "value for money" deal.'
—Simon Stenning, MCA Insight, UK eating and drinking out intelligence

Eating out is now seen as a form of entertainment and self-expression. This means that value for money can no longer be applied only to the cost of the meal. With phrases such as 'YOLO' (you only live once) and 'FOMO' (fear of missing out) becoming popular among consumers, it's obvious they value experiences over material possessions – and they're willing to pay for them. They're even willing to queue for hours for a unique experience.

You may have thought the days of standing in lines were over, but nowadays, it can be a status symbol – something to brag about to friends on social media. It fits the short-attention-span fascination with anything new to tell your friends that you're in the front line for an experience. Lining up is no longer a negative experience for either the brand or the customer. For example, in London, Barrafina, a Michelin-starred tapas bar that operates a no-booking policy, sees people queuing up for lengthy periods without complaint. This represents a huge cultural shift.

Since eating out is increasingly about creating experiences, it now involves feeding the soul as much as the belly. What defines 'value' is changing as customers seek a variety of sensory experiences across all categories and price points. It's no longer about offering the cheapest meal deal; it's much more multifaceted than that. Expecting non-tangible value for an out-of-home eating/drinking experience, consumers are willing to spend a little more. You need look no further for proof than the fact that today, people are willing to spend over £3 for a cup of coffee – unthinkable until quite recently – every single day.

The challenge this presents to the restaurant industry is that it's not always easy to offer your guests an experience with every meal, so knowing where to start and what the available options are is essential. Begin by understanding what it is the modern consumer is looking for, and then you can cater your offerings to suit their taste.

If your restaurant is currently offering similar menu choices to the other restaurants on the high street, if it has the same look and feel as any other chain in the country, you won't be special or unique enough to stand out from the crowd. With 'samey' casual dining outlets reaching saturation point, it's easy to see why they are going wrong when their guests are looking for places that reflect individuality.

Creating a unique experience isn't as difficult as it may at first seem – it's all about having a little imagination that will set you apart from the competition and grabbing the customers' attention.

Convenience

According to Mintel's 'Hot and Cold Cereal' report in 2017, modern consumers can even consider having cereal for breakfast a bit of an imposition because it leaves a dirty bowl. Millennials in particular are more used to seeking convenience than any other generation. Their time, and how it's used, has taken on a different meaning to them – if it's not instant, it's not worth it.

Essentially, the more portable a food item is, the more likely it is consumers will order it for breakfast or a snack. As a result, snacking all day long has become preferable to the traditional three meals a day.

In fact, it wasn't until the seventeenth century that breakfast started to be eaten regularly by most social classes. Its popularity then rose in the early twentieth century thanks to Mr Kellogg's accidental invention of cornflakes. Similarly, lunch only became part of the daily eating pattern of the masses during the Industrial Revolution when factory bosses realised workers needed midday sustenance in order to keep pace with their punishing workloads. Eating patterns are constantly evolving. The modern-day consumer's love of snacking – fuelled by hunger – is now regarded as healthier than eating three square meals per day, and there's little consumers love more than being able to use their smartphones or tablets to order ahead and pay online. This growing use of technology is also great news for marketers as they can use it to engage consumers with the brand, its story and the business values.

Health

'Diet' isn't to be confused with 'health'. Unless food is vegan, vegetarian, organic, sustainably-sourced or made with functional ingredients, consumers aren't likely to fall for the 'it's healthy' trick.

Consumers like to eat with their eyes, but these days, their hearts and minds play their parts, too. This may mean adapting what you buy in and inventory costs may increase as a result, but this will be balanced out by the fact that consumers are prepared to pay more for fresh, locally sourced food. Millennials are paving the way, wanting customisation to create their own unique healthy dishes. However, according to Mintel's report 'Millennials' Dining Habits', they also can't resist indulging themselves, and 17% of them feel like they're missing out on a little bit of naughtiness when they order healthy foods in a restaurant. That doesn't mean they'll order the biggest ice cream sundae or the stickiest toffee pudding for dessert. The key response for operators is to strike the perfect balance between healthy and indulgent foods, with the option to customise meals depending on their guests' moods and preferences.

Customisation

In a culturally rich and diverse UK, consumers consider themselves to be unique individuals now more than at any other time. They have more adventurous palates, and they actively seek out unusual ethnic flavours such as Chilean and Korean. In addition, they're attracted to a variety of ingredients so they can tailor their meals – more/less spice or seasoning, for example, or a choice of garnishes for drinks, from rosemary sprigs to edible flowers. In fact, 30% of young consumers say that being able to customise their meal or drink is an important factor when they're considering which restaurant to visit.

For the 'no-one-is-quite-like-me' demographic, new ways to customise are exciting. Therefore, it's in brands' best interests to take that mind-set on board in order to be seen as fresh and appealing.

Connections

Society is becoming rapidly detached from the real people who populate it. It's increasingly easy to shut ourselves away and disappear into the digital world. Friends connect more online than they do in person.

There is no doubt technology has allowed foodservice businesses to ensure accuracy, manage data, and improve the speed of service. After all, 38% of Britons, especially in the nineteen to twenty-eight age bracket, agree that it is faster to place orders using a self-service kiosk than at the counter, bypassing the need for human cashiers. The Mintel Trend 'Who Needs Humans?' examines the way in which machines are increasingly replacing people.

And yet, the loss of personal interaction has sparked a backlash against this trend, with 64% of Britons agreeing that human customer service is necessary to a pleasurable dining experience. Over forty-fives in particular demand a real connection (70% vs 58% of sixteen to forty-four-year-olds). Even if your outlet/restaurant has adopted self-order kiosks, it would be wise to give consumers the option to order at the counter.

We, as hospitality industry professionals, have a responsibility to encourage people to spend quality time with others, connecting over good food. It's refreshing to see more and more restaurants creating community seating areas to encourage young diners to expand their social circles and break bread with new friends, away from the tide of technology. Even single diners are being made to feel like welcome guests rather than social outcasts.

Far from being an impediment to real social interaction, though, technology can be a restaurant's biggest attraction.

- 77% of Millennials claim that technology improves their dining experience
- 49% of Millennials prefer digital receipts – text or email – to paper ones
- 63% appreciate the use of technology for ordering on server-handled tablets
- 60% would prefer to use mobile pay

(Source: Toast's 'Restaurant Technology' report, 2017)

Authenticity

Customers are increasingly aware of authenticity when it comes to a business's branding, values and community involvement. They like to connect with brands through corporate social responsibility initiatives, and they want to know which charities the brands support, and why. Do they recycle or implement responsible waste management? Customers also value brands that support local suppliers.

What exactly does this mean for your restaurant business? Authenticity can't be manufactured; it has to be a genuine reflection of who you are and what you stand for. Transparency is key, therefore, in how you communicate your values to your ever-curious customers, either online on in your restaurant. Remain honest about who you are and what you promise.

For example, when a customer checks out your social media presence (which they will) and your Facebook ads promote a fun, relaxed, family-friendly restaurant with a modern atmosphere, that's exactly what your guests will expect. Remain true to the promises of your messaging and avoid falling into the style over substance trap to maintain a certain image. Remember, you and your customers are real people, and they will appreciate a brand that is honest, relatable, and humorous whenever appropriate.

Why you need to embrace the experience economy

In 1999, when US business analysts Joseph Pine and James Gilmore first defined the concept of the experience economy, they noted that goods and services were no longer enough for consumers. Society was on the brink of moving from mass-market commodities towards more personalised and unique experiences. Pine and Gilmore predicted that in the near future, businesses would have to meet this demand and create memorable interactions and experiences to capture their audiences' imaginations. Therefore, they'd also need to transform their brands' value propositions. Pine and Gilmore were visionaries who foresaw that power would shift from the producers to the consumers.

They were right.

The experience economy has arrived. According to an Eventbrite 2017 survey, more than 75% of Millennials would choose to spend their money 'on a desirable experience or event rather than buying something desirable', while 55% state that they're spending more on events and live experiences than ever before.

The reasons for this are, in my opinion, clear. Millennials place great significance on creating life-long memories, not only from attending events and participating in live experiences, but also from having the ability to share these experiences with others via social media channels, both in real time and post event. It's now possible to engage and feel connected with anyone across the globe.

Eating out is seen as a form of entertainment. Pine and Gilmore argued, 'In a world saturated with largely undifferentiated goods and services, the greatest opportunity for value creation resides in staging experiences'. A bar, hotel or restaurant should be moving beyond competing on food, drinks and rooms, and should instead treat the entire business as if it were a stage on which all staff are performing. Guests can be encouraged to participate in that performance (passively or actively), thus transforming mundane interactions into vibrant, engaging and personalised encounters. This is the basis of the rapidly emerging experience economy, and its rise is taking the world by storm as spending and leisure habits are changing.

Now, more than ever, consumers desire unique, spontaneous and immersive experiences, no matter where they are, because these experiences form an integral part of self-expression and identity. The better the experience, the greater the satisfaction in sharing it with others. In these experiences, consumers are collecting memories. The only thing a material object collects, on the other hand, is dust.

In our fast-paced modern world, customers want more than just food and drink when they choose to dine in your restaurant. To capture this market, you not only need to make sure your central product is of the highest quality, you also need to design your business around creating experiences and tailoring them to your audience.

At one time, if we wanted to watch our favourite TV programme, we'd all have to sit down at the same time on the same day and watch it on the same channel. Streaming and on-demand video services have revolutionised the broadcasting industry, and I would argue that the experience economy is having the same effect on the restaurant trade. Diners across the generations no longer want to follow the old rules and be exposed to the ways of the past. In all areas of social culture, people need stimulation and crave a variety of experiences on demand. Furthermore, they are willing to pay a premium in return. But these experiences need to be carefully designed/staged, and always bespoke to the customers' needs, saying something unique about them and their choices.

It's essential, therefore, that the hospitality business becomes guest-centric beyond the primary offering of food, drinks, tables and rooms. No touchpoints with your guests – from your online reservations page right through to them arriving at reception, ordering at the bar, even going to the bathroom – can be left to chance. You and all your staff need the customer to believe that a whole world of possibilities for remarkable bespoke interactions has opened up for them the moment they make contact with your business. The sum of extraordinary interactions across the business is much greater than its individual parts, and the overall enjoyment you create will translate into a memorable experience that will be firmly imprinted on your customer's mind. It's like watching a fantastic movie and feeling overwhelmed by the end of it – no way will you remember all the lines, but the experience and the emotions it evoked mean that movie will stand out in your mind more than the generic chick-flick you wish you hadn't bothered with the week before.

At some point in a restaurant's lifetime (the sooner, the better), it will likely want to offer customers the sense that they're experiencing something unique.

'Unless companies want to be in a commoditized business, they will be compelled to upgrade their offerings to the next stage of economic value. The question, then, isn't whether, but when – and how – to enter the emerging experience economy.'
—The Harvard Business Review

CASE STUDY – STREET FEAST

I've noticed on many occasions how people change their dining habits when something new and different arrives on the scene. For example, when a street food outlet opens up, people gravitate towards it and away from existing reliable casual dining outlets. It's not because they've suddenly lost their appetite for tried and trusted dishes served in a clean environment; instead, they're drawn to the new multisensory experiences of unusual flavours, the element of surprise, and the more spontaneous human interaction. It doesn't matter if the whole street food experience is rather chaotic and they wait in long queues; they're happy to drink in the noise and feel the air filling their nostrils with aromatic smells. It shouldn't work, by traditional standards, but it does – and it's a growing trend.

A prime example is London Union's Street Feast, ostensibly a collection of street food markets also offering drinks and music. Its ambience encourages sharing and culinary exploration, introducing a communal aspect to the fray. With nightclubbing on the decline as a leisure activity, late-night street food markets are appealing to the younger generations as a new and exciting alternative.

Street Feast, by its co-founder Jonathon Downey's own admission, is about 'getting a load of people in a car park to try things out'. Mass market it's not, with its quirky, individual feel and its old shipping containers, 'dirty' food and burning oil drums. However, it has struck a chord with its consumer base, which is completely aligned to Street Feast's offering.

It just goes to show that a good dining experience isn't about white tablecloths, the finest wines, or multi-million-pound décor. Street Feast embodies creative thinking, ingenuity, careful planning, and an eye for building something that can't be bought elsewhere. Ultimately, it creates a unique experience, shareable by its customers via social media. And 60% of Millennials, 45% of people aged thirty-five to forty-four, and 34% of people aged between forty-five and fifty-four say their experiences are improved when they can share them on social media.

CASE STUDY – STARBUCKS

Starbucks is my favourite brand, and it's one I've studied closely for decades. I've had a long-standing working relationship with coffee, and the Starbucks story has played a pivotal role in my understanding of the experience economy.

I found it fascinating to study declining worldwide coffee sales when the industry stagnated because it was competing on price only. My arrival in the UK from Poland in the early nineties was an eye opener as it provided me with a piece of missing insight which demonstrated how an established category, even in decline, could be turned around. For the first time, I saw Starbucks coffee shops, with their modern approach to service, focus on customer experience and bespoke coffee products – 87,000 ways you can order your drinks at Starbucks? Mind-boggling!

It was way back in 1987 when Howard Schultz entered the coffee business and bought out Starbucks (founded 1973) with one goal in mind: to enhance the personal relationship between people and their coffee. His life, and in turn the business of coffee, changed forever when Schultz went on a business trip to Milan. There he encountered several espresso bars, and to his amazement, the bar owners knew their customers by name and served them bespoke drinks such as cappuccinos and café lattés the way they liked them. Schultz had an epiphany the moment he understood that people could – and did – have a personal relationship with coffee.

Schultz's ambition for Starbucks was to cultivate an Italian-style experience for coffee-lovers, but this was rejected by Starbucks' founders. He spoke to 242 investors, and 217 of them said no. Nobody believed that the concept of bespoke coffee (with a price tag three times higher than any other café in the USA), served in 'on-the-go' paper cups, could present a viable business opportunity.

However, he persisted, and the rest is history. The whole world fell in love with Starbucks, and by 2017 sales had reached $22,4bn with 13,930 outlets in operation in the USA and 27,339 worldwide. The sceptics who once doubted Starbucks could charge more than $2 per cup were proved wrong, with customers happily paying $4–$5 on a regular basis.

Pushing the boundaries even further, the brand is launching a series of upscale outlets known as 'Starbucks Reserve' with manual espresso machines and four different types of brewing methods, allowing consumers to tailor their beverage to their exact preference. Targeting consumers with an appetite for personalised premium coffee, these Instagram-inspired beverages will be priced at up to $12 per cup. Will it work? Of course it will!

Starbucks's success is rooted in its mission to serve great coffee, offering quality service in an environment that is cool and comfortable to hang out in. It embraces the experience economy to the fullest. How special is the ritual of writing your name on a Starbucks's cap to make it uniquely yours?

And Starbucks continues to evolve as a brand, listening and responding to its customers' changing habits. In recent years, Starbucks has broadened its product range beyond warm beverages to include snacks, cakes, packaged coffees and tea. It even provides coffee-making equipment and merchandise such as branded mugs, all designed to help boost its sales.

Starbucks combines the concepts of guest-centricity, customisation, innovation, experimentation, social media visibility/accessibility, customer engagement and on-trend market research. The results are key outcomes of both its brand and its marketing strategy.

It's also worth noting that throughout his career, Schultz has always prioritised his employees (including part-time workers), whom he calls 'partners', offering them complete health-care and stock options. This is a concept I will be discussing in more detail in Chapter 4.

Make the experience economy work for you

Starbucks demonstrates that premium processes can work for products, or even entire categories, that apply consistent quality to a valuable personal experience. Great experiences make a tangible impact on the business and contribute to its commercial success. The experience economy is a global trend affecting all industries as people increasingly value experiences above anything else.

You may now be asking, 'What do I need to do? How will I know this experience economy will work for my business?' I know that we can't all be Starbucks and have access to its marketing funds and resources. But the principles behind its success don't simply apply to multi-national corporations; they apply to us all. If we don't get to know the customers who will be our biggest future market, it's only going to get tougher to stay afloat. The information to help us understand what's happening is out there and we all need to take note.

PWC's 2018 report 'Experience is Everything: Here's how to get it right' states that:

- 73% of all people point to customer experience as an important factor in their purchasing decisions

- 43% of all consumers would pay more for greater convenience

- 42% would pay more for a friendly, welcoming experience
- 65% find having a positive customer experience with a brand to be more influential than great advertising

Nearly every industry can achieve a potential price hike in return for providing a positive customer experience, and hospitality establishments can benefit massively from providing a top-flight service. The key to their success will be making their customers' experiences unique and bespoke to their market.

The good news is that human nature drives our desire to experiment. This in turn creates more opportunities for experience-based businesses, such as hotels, bars and restaurants, to increase their business value. Nearly every outlet, be it a local pub, an independent coffee shop, a fine-dining restaurant or a boutique hotel, can provide an extra layer of intangible value beyond the business's basic function, regardless of its price positioning.

People will always crave something memorable; they want to create and collect memories through an experience they can connect with – something that makes them feel like a participant and not just a bystander. In the next chapter, I'll show you how to make this happen for your customers by mapping their journey as they encounter all the key touchpoints that you need to deliver remarkable bespoke experiences.

CHAPTER TWO

Experiences Must Become Your Product

After forty-five minutes of waiting in line, Dan and Zoë are invited into the restaurant. Its warm, welcoming tones are complemented by a buzz of chatter and laughter, and the couple feel excited as to what lies ahead of them.

To Zoë's amazement, the waiter greets them by name and wishes her a happy birthday. As they hand over their coats, cold and damp from the winter night outside, Zoë turns to Dan with a big smile on her face.

I've placed this chapter here as a measure of its importance. It sets the scene for the rest of the book, summarising all the key touchpoints, interactions and experiences on the table above and beyond food and drink. I'll be discussing the whole eating out experience, from the moment the customer considers booking a venue – even if it's just a vague idea to go out with their friends – to the point it becomes a plan and they start searching around for the right venue. What is it they're looking for? Is the meeting a celebration? What does your venue offer and what does it deliver? What type of food and drinks fit the bill?

Once the customer has made their decision, based on a whole menu of variables, they make their booking. From this point forward, all the meaningful interactions between the customer and the venue begin. First impressions count, from the moment the customer arrives outside the venue, to the welcome inside and the feel, look and smell of the restaurant, the cloakrooms, even the toilets. Who would have thought that your loo would be rated alongside your vindaloo?

Eating out for today's diners isn't just about the food and drink; it's become a multisensory information-loaded experience, and everything – from the music, the seating arrangements, the flowers, to the way a steak is prepared and cooked – is just as important as the actual food. Each individual element contributes to the whole picture and the impressions your business makes on the customer.

The time when offering great food was good enough has gone. Dining out is now a connected experience for the customer, from the initial idea right through to receiving a personalised email from the restaurant three months later, offering to welcome them back again with their favourite cocktail ready and waiting. If that surprises you, then I'm not surprised – it's one of the reasons I've been prompted to write this book. It used to be the fly in the soup that ruined a diner's evening; now, it can be the fact your chicken isn't free range, organic and local, or your cocktails are served with a plastic straw – that really irks the customer.

If your restaurant isn't already personalised and connected to your customers, then this chapter will offer you some serious food for thought. The customers' experience of your restaurant or bar starts way before they arrive. In fact, they're likely to have formed an impression of your venue before they even step through the door, gleaned from social media, star ratings and forums that make it easy for new customers to talk to strangers about your establishment before they talk to you. If your décor needs refreshing, your lighting is wrong, or the music you play isn't up to scratch, people will talk about it in an instant, and that can either make or break your reputation.

Making the necessary changes to attract your customers needn't cost the earth. Even if you only run a single venue, you still face competition from the big players. You might not be able to compete on price, but fear not – cheap eats are on their way out, and 'quality' is in. For 'quality', however, read 'experience'.

The stakes are high

It doesn't matter if you run a small family café or a Michelin-starred restaurant, the quality of the overall experience is just as important to your guests as the food. Value for money is being redefined and what you sell beyond what's prepared in the kitchen will dictate the price you can charge.

Data shows that consumers are dining out less often, but when they do, they are prepared to pay more for a venue offering them a memorable experience beyond the food. On that basis, you can afford to charge more per portion, as long as your core proposition meets your customers' expectations, delivering an experience of some sort which informs their sense of value for money.

For example, you might have a long-standing reputation for serving great steak, yet over a period of time, your daily covers have fallen away. Not even dropping your prices has improved things. That's because your customers' habits are evolving. The competition stakes have changed, but the story around your steak hasn't. It's still the same old (albeit tasty) steak.

What if you were to add a little seasoning to your story? How would that improve your situation? For example, you could continue to sell the same great steak, but you add details such as:

- Your meat is organic and supplied by a long-standing local family butcher +

- The side orders are customised +

- Bespoke cocktails +

- Food theatre (eg hot stone cooking, smoking chambers, open kitchen) +

- Knowledgeable service +

- Striking venue design +

- 'Eatertainment' (live music, events, theme nights, etc)

Now you're not just selling great food, you're running an experiential venue, and thus you will be able to mark-up the costs by between 20–40%. Plus, you'll be standing out from the crowd, so not only will your food be an attraction, but your experiential offering will grab the attention of a customer base keen to upscale their dining experience.

This is an essential shift of mind-set that I would urge *all* restaurant owners and brands to engage with. Don't risk your longevity by sticking with your usual margins. Instead, think about the story that lies behind your offering. The story then becomes part of the overall experience that will have your customers leaving glowing reviews online and coming back for more. Of course, food quality isn't up for discussion – get that wrong and you're toast.

Ask yourself, whether you're struggling to keep afloat or filling your restaurant on a regular basis, what experiences you can create. As the leading out-of-home food and drinks data and research company, CGA, revealed in its 'Business Leaders' Survey' in 2018, 81% of business leaders see quality of experience as a key driver for consumers when they're choosing where to eat or drink out. In today's competitive market, it's vital, therefore, to consider how you can extend your customer experience to attract your target demographic.

Providing a customer experience isn't an alien concept in the hospitality trade; hotels have been leading the way for some time. It's not unusual for guests to begin their hotel experience by boarding a complimentary shuttle service to and from the airport. Longer staying guests enjoy enhanced concierge services tailored to their needs, such as organised excursions and events away from the hotel.

Shopping malls are also increasingly providing hassle-free valet parking to reduce shoppers' stress. Most airlines allow travellers to check in remotely via apps or print boarding passes to facilitate a smoother travel experience at the airport.

The one thing that unites these super initiatives is that they all extend the customer experience *beyond* the main event – be that staying overnight, shopping, or travelling – thereby facilitating a better experience once the customer arrives. The restaurant trade will,

I guarantee, head more and more in this direction, probably sooner than we may think.

For most consumers, booking a restaurant is a form of escapism from everyday life, offering opportunities to party, spend quality time with family and friends, or simply to take a coffee break. For the corporate customer, restaurants are ideal for conducting a business meeting. Whatever the reason for the visit, once the customer has made the decision to eat out, the planning process begins. They will be asking themselves questions such as:

- Where shall I go?
- How far am I prepared to travel?
- How much can I spend?
- What venues will accommodate my dietary requirements?
- What is the right venue for the occasion?
- Is it appropriate for a meeting with business partners to negotiate a new deal?

Before the guests arrive, their experience has begun, and their impressions go beyond the quality of the food.

CASE STUDY –
'HONEY, I LEFT THE KIDS BEHIND'

Often, the USA leads the way with customer service when innovation is key to a brand's success in an over-saturated market. With so many similar choices, brands are increasingly adopting new ways to extend their restaurant experience beyond the table. One such brand is the chain of Olive Garden restaurants.

This chain identified a gap in its sector market, in which it had been attempting to compete by changing its menus to appeal to families. The question it asked was, 'What do mums and dads really want from a dining experience?'

The resulting campaign was one I can only describe as genius. Olive Garden recognised that on Valentine's Night, most parents found it difficult to eat out together without their kids. The reality for most parents was that organising childcare on such a busy night of the year, when singleton teens weren't really up for babysitting, was almost impossible. In response, Olive Garden partnered with the nationwide My Gym children's fitness centres. My Gym would offer a free babysitting service as long as the parents made a reservation at one of Olive Garden's restaurants. At a single stroke, this partnership removed all the hassle of organising childcare and freed up parents in their thousands to enjoy a well-deserved 'date night' at an Olive Garden venue.

I applaud this creativity. Olive Garden understood what it needed to do to drive increased targeted sales, and as a result, connected directly with the customers' needs beyond the food offering. The campaign itself was 'liked' 163,370 on Facebook and shared nearly 7,000 times. In the context of social media, this was a very successful promotion.

How well do you know your existing customers? Indeed, how well do you know your prospects, and what can you do to reach them in today's market?

Where to start

Creating a connected experience is about ensuring your guests enjoy interacting with you. That includes offering them not only food and drinks that they will love, but also opportunities to understand what your brand represents and how it aligns to their values. And that extends to providing impeccable service at every interaction level, right through to ensuring that the venue design and space, inside and outside, are fit for purpose, enabling your guests to enjoy quality moments, no matter the occasion, or what type of venue you provide.

From a café to fast-casual, all the way to fine dining, if your guests want coffee, then it has to be the best. A burger needs to be the most experiential burger in the world, and a £35 cocktail needs to blow their socks off with all the magic that the bartender can pull out of the hat. No sector in the market is immune to this level of quality and service.

The immediate steps you can take are to:

- Listen
- Be open minded
- Be objective

Firstly, listen to your staff, because they're on the front line and interact with your customers all the time. Your staff will be the first ones to tell you if your guests – the customers – are unhappy. And guests can be unhappy about a whole range of things – anything from being delayed to the cleanliness of your cutlery and glassware. And if your cocktails are substandard, forget it!

Your staff are key people who drive the success of your business, and their ability to recognise, action and prevent major weaknesses in the guests' journey will be vital for not only ensuring quality, but also driving sales. Staff are your eyes and ears and represent your brand on the floor. If they don't get what you're about, you need to step up your game and offer them the right training.

I'll explain the importance of staff in more detail in Chapter 4.

Secondly, pay careful attention to what customers are saying about you on social media, while remaining objective. Don't simply dismiss customers' negative comments on the grounds that you believe you serve great food and drinks, and your guests must have been bad tempered on the night.

Finally, ask your guests questions directly. After all, dining out is generally a social experience, and you're looking to create experiences that people will want to talk about. Encourage your guests to offer their feedback not just on your food and drinks, but also on the environment you've created, from the seating arrangements, the lighting, the music, to the cloakrooms. Invite them to tell you what they think could benefit from improvement. These are simple, but important, questions. The responses you receive from say fifty or more guests will show opinion trends, providing you with important insights into the customer roadmap and whether you need to implement any changes.

Whatever you do, don't resent negative feedback; instead, consider how you might overcome it. Remain objective and capture all the feedback, whether you like it or not, and notice any recurring patterns.

Mapping your customers' journey

'A customer journey map is a very simple idea: a diagram that illustrates the steps your customer(s) go through in engaging with your company, whether it be a product, an online experience, retail experience, or a service, or any combination. The more touchpoints you have, the more complicated – but necessary – such a map becomes.'
—Harvard Business Review (November, 2010)

Getting your customer journey right across all key touchpoints is vital. Since experience is everything in hospitality, you need to design bespoke approaches at every stage.

TOUCH POINTS PRE-VISIT

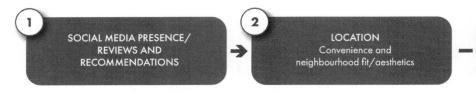

1 SOCIAL MEDIA PRESENCE/ REVIEWS AND RECOMMENDATIONS → **2** LOCATION Convenience and neighbourhood fit/aesthetics —

TOUCH POINTS AT VENUE

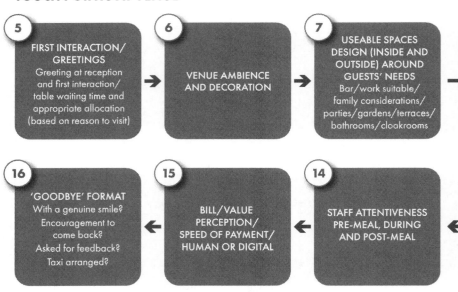

5 FIRST INTERACTION/ GREETINGS Greeting at reception and first interaction/ table waiting time and appropriate allocation (based on reason to visit) → **6** VENUE AMBIENCE AND DECORATION → **7** USEABLE SPACES DESIGN (INSIDE AND OUTSIDE) AROUND GUESTS' NEEDS Bar/work suitable/ family considerations/ parties/gardens/terraces/ bathrooms/cloakrooms —

16 'GOODBYE' FORMAT With a genuine smile? Encouragement to come back? Asked for feedback? Taxi arranged? ← **15** BILL/VALUE PERCEPTION/ SPEED OF PAYMENT/ HUMAN OR DIGITAL ← **14** STAFF ATTENTIVENESS PRE-MEAL, DURING AND POST-MEAL ←

TOUCH POINTS POST-VISIT

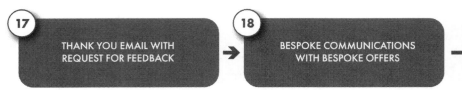

17 THANK YOU EMAIL WITH REQUEST FOR FEEDBACK → **18** BESPOKE COMMUNICATIONS WITH BESPOKE OFFERS —

Figure 2.1 Mapping Your Customers

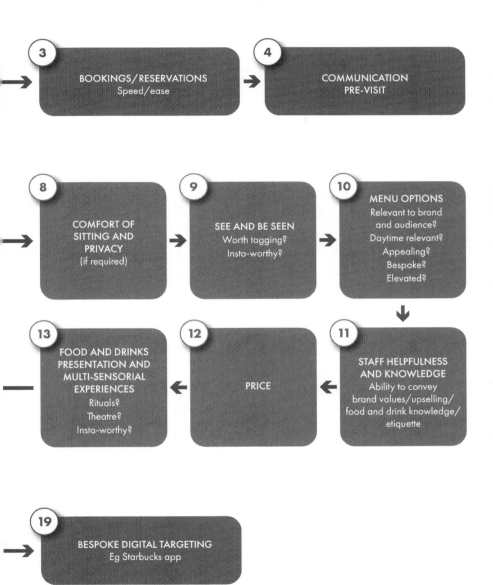

Mapping your customers' journey needn't involve sophisticated software or skills. You can begin by asking questions in relation to the various touchpoints they interact with, as shown in the diagram.

This figure is a simple representation of your guests' journey before, during and after their visit. While there might be some sector variations at different stages (eg, with a coffee outlet, its location will be the first consumer consideration), overall, the process and touchpoints remain the same.

If customer journey mapping isn't a process you've carried out before, I highly recommend that you do so. It will offer you valuable insights, and you may even discover things about the journey that you don't like yourself, but you've never paid enough attention to them before. If that's the case, you can't expect your customers to like them, either.

Guest journey mapping isn't a one-off exercise; it needs to become part of your standard practice because, like your customers, it's a living, evolving thing that's affected by mood, personality and the world in general. Adjust your customer journey maps on a monthly, or at the very least a quarterly, basis in order to answer the questions:

- How can we add more value to our customers at each step of this journey?

- How can we help customers at each stage achieve their goals more easily?

The customers' path to purchase is formed of:

- How they behave, pre and post visit

- Where they go

- How they socialise

- What other places they considered prior to choosing your venue

This path presents valuable opportunities for a restaurant or hotel. Mapping the consumers' journey in this way will help you understand the key moments that influence their decision making. Although it can be a lengthy process, it's worth taking the time and effort to get it right before you define the paths that different types of customers can take to spend their money with you.

Once you have your customers' journey mapped, the next step is to identify their highs and lows at each interaction with your brand. Knowing this will clearly demonstrate where you need to improve.

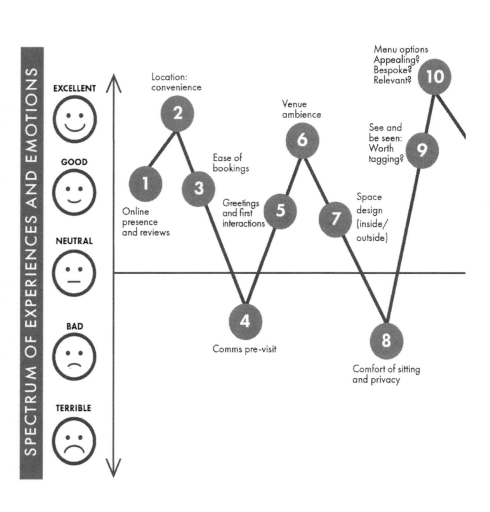

Figure 2.2 Restaurant X: Guests' experience journey

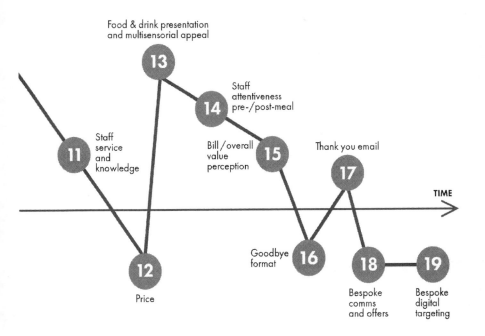

Mapping your guests' experience

A customer's experience with your brand is all about their journey and how you interact with them. The only way to bring that journey to life reliably is by continuously capturing data.

Again, this does not require expensive, complicated software; just listen to your customers, encourage their honest feedback and allow this to open your eyes. Check their reviews on platforms such as TripAdvisor, social media and – dare I say it? – talk to them face to face. Capture feedback that relates to the relevant touchpoints of the journey and learn what you can from your sales data.

Loyalty programmes are fantastic ways to aggregate customer data, and sophisticated analytics techniques can turn this data into powerful insights. Often, though, you will already subconsciously know what works well and what can be improved in your restaurant.

From this graphic we can see that Restaurant X's food and drinks offering is exceptional, the space and design of the venue is not far from perfect, but the seating arrangement, size of tables and space between them needs work to create more privacy and comfort. We can also see that staff knowledge and attentiveness could be improved, but more urgently, the welcome/goodbye experience must be addressed, since the guests' pre and postexperience interactions register as a big let-down. First and last impressions are what the customer will take away from your venue.

Key data capture

'Next-generation customers are... hyper connected, and if a location lets them use technology to place an order, they'll come back 6 percent more often and spend 20 percent more each time, according to our survey results. They value connections, and 70 percent of survey respondents look for apps that deliver personalized offers and convey the sense that a restaurant "knows them".'
—Deloitte's 'Restaurant of the Future' survey, 2016

This is a highly valuable insight into the way consumers' mind-sets are heading. I'm convinced that a truly personalised guest experience is what we must all be striving to deliver, because such an approach will drive real loyalty and revenue. Therefore, tailored marketing communication clearly presents significant opportunities for a restaurant to connect directly with its customers.

We must ask ourselves, 'How often do customers today end up communicating with an automated robot with zero personality? Is this really the way forward in engaging with them?' There are benefits, of course, to technology, but how it's used will make all the difference.

For example, capturing the right data in compliance with GDPR (general data protection regulation), you can build a picture of your customers. In this context, it's important you ensure that, from the basic information you collect, combined with you customers' preferences, you create a story from which to deliver their experience.

The right data includes:

- Contact info: name, address, email, phone number

- Demographic: gender, age, nationality

- Usage history: reason for visit, occasion, number of visits, average spend, with friends/family/business colleagues

- Food and drink preferences: foodie, meat eater/pescatarian/vegetarian/vegan, allergies, alcoholic drink preference – spirits/wine/cocktails/teetotal, dessert choice, digestives/aperitifs

- Space preferences: upstairs/downstairs/terrace, quiet corner, table by the window, wi-fi/electrical socket/access to a printer

- Experiential: feedback from reviews, prior surveys, comments made to the staff

With this data at your fingertips, you can employ it across all touchpoints to improve the customer journey and open up experiences like never before. It will also be invaluable to your staff in:

- Determining guests' dietary requirements and allergies

- Encouraging repeat business by offering bespoke options

- Sharing menu items

- Emphasising locally sourced produce for guests who care about food provenance

Post visit, your marketing team could then invite guests to a new menu launch, or to attend exclusive events, from celebrity-guest performance nights to the opening of outdoor dining in a redesigned garden.

For more sophisticated data analysis, there are dozens of inexpensive technology platforms which offer specialist solutions integrating multiple systems, from booking data capture, enquiries and EPOS (electronic point of sale), to loyalty schemes, and bringing them together in a single dashboard. Data and feedback can also be repurposed via social media and online reviews that you can leverage, leading to truly personalised guest experiences. Over time, you'll establish quality relationships with guests who will feel welcome in your establishment by having their unique preferences appreciated.

Without doubt, the restaurant industry is transforming, and competition is more intense than ever before. The 'winning' restaurant brands will be those that understand their guests, improve their design to reflect their brand or theme, capitalise on digital technology and analytics, and seize the opportunity to engage customers in a highly personalised way. The solution, as this book sets out, is bespoke.

Touchpoints

Whether you own a bar, restaurant, coffee shop or fast-food outlet, the guests' journey won't differ dramatically. However, the touchpoints will have varying levels of significance relative to both your offering and your customer expectations.

For example, a thirty-minute wait for a freshly prepared meal at a fine-dining venue is accepted as the norm, but it's completely unacceptable in a casual fast-food outlet ('fast' being the operative word). Five-star hotels are expected to be furnished stylishly with luxuriously stocked bathrooms, while for a café, a simple design and an outstanding level of cleanliness is fine. However, it's vital that you're fully aware of what your touchpoints mean to the customer in respect to your venue – ignore them at your peril!

To help you understand the importance that customers attach to your touchpoints, I've grouped them into six distinct categories:

- Your brand and company culture

- Employees

- Customer service

- Elevated food and drinks

- Space and interior design

- Technology and marketing

We'll examine each category in more detail in the following chapters. Each must be carefully evaluated to fit your brand's mission/personality, then tailored to your guests' needs.

CASE STUDY – PIZZAEXPRESS

PizzaExpress was founded by Peter Boizot in Wardour Street, London, in 1965. A firm UK high-street favourite and household name, it's also an international brand with over 600 restaurants globally and a reach into supermarkets.

The company credits much of its success to continually innovating what it offers to its loyal customer base, as well as cooking fantastic pizzas. It was one of the first restaurant chains to adopt open kitchens, and it constantly strives to create memorable experiences at every touchpoint. Today, it offers an online 'click and collect' service and has partnered with Deliveroo and Just Eat to offer home delivery.

For every touchpoint the customer interacts with, the company has tried to make the process as easy and seamless as possible. This has entailed building a bespoke 'behind-the-scenes' bookings and table management system which integrates online and telephone reservations.

In constantly listening to its customers, PizzaExpress carried out a survey which revealed that 69% of customers found the most frustrating part of eating out in the brand's restaurants was waiting to pay their bill. PizzaExpress responded and introduced its own app which allows customers to pay and go in under a minute. However, the app goes one step further, allowing groups to split the bill easily, which was another friction point.

Timothy Love, Senior Marketing Manager of PizzaExpress, is on record as saying that the brand is always on the lookout for ways in which it can improve its customers' experiences, and that the 'pay at table' app was the perfect solution for those customers who would rather spend time eating their pizza than sorting out the bill. In listening to its customers, PizzaExpress showed how important touchpoints are along the way.

In 2017, PizzaExpress realised that many of its customers were using Facebook to book restaurants via the Messenger app. Responding to this trend, the PizzaExpress team developed a 24/7 fully integrated 'chat bot' to walk customers through the booking on this platform as a way of reducing time and effort for customers on the go. As a result, a host of industry awards followed, complete with massive media coverage. The chat bot also successfully appealed to a new demographic not previously captured by the brand. While PizzaExpress has no plans to dispense with human interaction completely, chat bots provide a speedier process that's been proven to meet the needs of prospects and convert them into customers.

In its drive to innovate, PizzaExpress has expanded its experiential offerings. Already known for hosting jazz in its London's Dean Street restaurant, it's looking to increase the scope of its live music entertainment with the conversion of fifty selected restaurants. Artists like Goldie, Gareth Gates and Martin Kemp (from Spandau Ballet) have all played for PizzaExpress in its London Holborn venue as the brand trials this option, with a view to expanding further into providing comedy or other performance-related nights.

Innovation is one of PizzaExpress's key drivers in differentiating itself from other pizza chains. The brand is unafraid to experiment and implement many of the ideas expressed in Deloitte's 'Restaurant of the Future' report, focusing on how to serve its customers at the different touchpoints on each customer's journey.

Bringing it all together

The first step for restaurants is to map customers' journeys to see what makes them mad and what excites them. Then they need to capture their guests' data to understand and build key audience and individual guest profiles. The third step is to score the experiences and emotions their guests are experiencing objectively, at the same time creating personalised communications at different touchpoints. The final step is for each staff member to have access to all available information about the guests whenever they need it.

Mapping the customer journey in this way is a powerful tool that will provide you, your company and your people with a greater understanding of your guests' needs and the key areas of potential opportunity. Knowledge is power, so make sure you can answer the following:

- Who are your guests and what are they looking for?

- What are your guests' requirements/concerns?

- How do they research your product/service, and what device do they use to do so?

- What are the criteria that help them to make a reservation?

- Which of your competitors' sites do they visit while evaluating places to eat out?

- Why do they choose your website, what is their experience of it, and can it be improved?

- What are their experiences while at your restaurant and how can they be improved?

- How easy is it for them to share their experiences on social media and give feedback during or after the event?

- Do they connect with you after the event, eg by reacting to/sharing website content such as recipes, tips, and seasonal offers?

In Deloitte's view, restaurants should take a broad view of the customer experience and 'wisely integrate the new digital capabilities people expect with the traditional comfort and value they have associated with restaurant experiences for generations'. I would echo this, along with a word of warning from Joe Ruiz of Strategic Marketing Solutions that 'today's differentiating innovation is tomorrow's universal expectation'. Only with a constant and rigorous focus on delivering the personalised experience at each and every touchpoint will your business succeed.

THE EXPERT'S OPINION
– JAMES HACON –

When it comes to technology and hospitality, there are many different schools of thought. At one end of the scale are the traditionalists, who see the need to preserve hospitality as an art form, mastered by the very talented. Some restaurateurs will argue until they are blue in the face that front-of-house technology takes away the magic. At the other end of the spectrum are those who believe that technology could eventually replace people altogether, with fully automated kitchens and robot waiters. One step further would be the *Star Trek* style food synthesizer, which is of course in the realms of possibility given the 3D food printers already on the market.

Technology will undoubtedly impact the future of hospitality, but the key will be ensuring it optimises the guest experience. The suitability of technology is highly linked to the occasion of a customer's dining experience. In the case of a quick lunch, where time pressure encourages grab-and-go, picking up a pre-packaged item and self-scanning feels like a great use of technology. This technology is already employed heavily in the supermarket industry and is beginning to find its way into food outlets.

On the other hand, if we take an occasion when a customer is looking for a memorable dining experience, then technology should be supporting a team of great servers in being more efficient and providing a personalised service. This could be in the form of brilliant guest history and information provided by a reservation system, digital menus to ease selection of dishes relating to allergies, or tablets at the table to help customers request more drinks when they are ready.

The one pain point that guests raise most often in-restaurant research is waiting for the bill. As the last interaction of the in-restaurant experience, it should be seamless, but this just isn't the case. Customers are often left waiting in their attempts to catch the server's attention.

Many technology providers have tried solving this and have, for the most part, failed in commercialising their solution. The latest iterations seem to be breaking through, but it's slow. One success story, however, is the Asian-inspired brand Wagamama, with its Wagamamago mobile app designed to allow guests to order additional items after their main order and pay their bill without seeing a server. The team carefully defined the functionality to ensure that it aligns to the brand's existing customer journey, with real-life interaction with a team member enabling its use.

The customer journey doesn't start and end at the restaurant door, but from the moment they are inspired to visit the venue to the moment they stop sharing their experience. However, restaurateurs often overlook the booking stage in the guest journey. Through my experience, I've identified that the customer's initial call response rate in restaurant groups is traditionally very low, dictated by poor staffing levels and service patterns. The majority of callers simply do not get through – which of course is not a great initial interaction. The use of technology is vital in hospitality, giving customers the choice as to whether they want to use it or not. In my experience, the majority of guests would still prefer to pick up the phone to book a restaurant.

James Hacon is Managing Director of Think Hospitality, which advises multi-site brands on growth and development strategy, as well as investing in early-stage concepts with a bright future.

CHAPTER THREE

Your Brand and Company Culture

In this chapter, I'll be discussing the key points you need to consider when it comes to creating your dream restaurant or bar. I really want you to stand out from the crowd and create the best possible experience for your customers when they visit.

It's important to think about the whole picture, particularly with a new venture, or if you're intending to refresh or rebrand your existing one. Think about how your great idea will translate into a going concern, from its location, its looks and feel, to what you'll be serving up on your menu. How will you communicate your values and what you stand for in ways that will attract new customers from the bar or bistro around the corner and keep them coming through your doors on a regular basis?

By following my advice, you'll understand why I place so much emphasis on gaining clarity from the outset with regards to the big picture, while never losing sight of the inspiration behind your passion.

Are you blinded by your vision?

You've had a great idea and you're burning to open a new restaurant or bar. Or perhaps it's time to refresh the place you currently run. Your enthusiasm is running high, you feel inspired to put your money where your mouth is, and you can't wait to welcome your guests to your tables.

Maybe you've just returned from a trip where you were blown away by *that* tapas bar on the beach, serving simple but gorgeously tasty small plates of food along with inexpensive fruity wines. Maybe on a city break you discovered the perfect bar with its cool ambience, mood lighting, roof terrace, unusual cocktails and no shortage of excited punters. Or perhaps it was an upscale 'anyone who's anyone' restaurant with its long list of the well-heeled waiting for its gourmet experience and wines that cost the earth. No matter what type of establishment ignited your passion – be it fast/casual/ fine dining – you're ready to take the plunge.

I applaud your passion, but the real work begins now.

The best ideas are always born from true passion; the next steps are to translate this passion into a vision, and then work out how to make your vision into a reality that is a reflection of you. My strongest advice at this stage of your brand's development is to take heed of these wise words: 'to thine own self be true'.

Right now, you're at the centre of everything, and the excitement you feel is dying to burst out from inside you. You're in the driving seat, the ideas and possibilities are forming in your head, and you just want to get on with it. Your vision is becoming clearer and you're picturing a steady stream of customers being wowed by what you've created. However, right now, your biggest investment isn't cash; it's you.

Before any great athlete powers forward to win Olympic gold, they've already invested in themselves and calculated exactly what event is the best fit for them. It's not just a matter of knowing they can perform on the track in the face of stiff competition; it's about the belief that they can win. When their passion, drive, natural talent, dedication and strategic planning come together as one, they'll be on the podium with the gongs around their neck, waving to their cheering fans. That's the difference they've been striving for so that they can win.

Yours may be a different type of competition, but it's still a competition. To be honest, you'll never win everyone over with what you do – and that's OK.

However, you will need a large number of committed fans who love what you do and cheer you on.

The one thing the world definitely doesn't need is another venue that's exactly the same as the one next door. You need to put your brand values and company culture at the heart of everything you do so that you can create the difference the world is looking for. Believe that what you're planning will create a memorable bespoke experience for your customers, communicated in a simple and clear way.

They came, they ate, they drank, you closed

Having a great idea for an exciting new brand isn't enough if you haven't done your market research. It's vitally important to ensure that your offering will appeal to prospects, its location is viable, and customers will visit you in the numbers you require to make it profitable.

Let's imagine that you've recently returned from a fantastic holiday and you're inspired by a particular venue where you drank cocktails as the sun set. You're telling yourself, 'I could do that.'

As it happens, there's a vacant building nearby which you think would be the perfect venue for your own bar. You're already pretty good at making cocktails and you're keen to try some new variations at home on your friends, along with a few tapas style snacks. Of course, they rave about your creations, and hey presto, that's your research complete. You're now the cocktail king or queen of your postcode.

Encouraged by your success, you enter into negotiations with landlords on the nitty gritty of the lease and endure the painstaking rigmarole of applying for and winning the expensive 'change of use' agreement from the council, including a late licence. You sign the lease, spend a small fortune fitting the building out, buy in your alcohol and formalise your 'little bites' menu. You're ready to open!

The first weekend, with much local fanfare, your friends arrive in droves to support you, along with a few curious locals. It proves to be a great start, and come Monday, you sit back and wait. However, this turns into a long wait. On weekdays, business is slow, while your expenditure is more than your income. You're at a loss to know what's gone wrong. After all, your friends have told you that your offering is 'brilliant'. The question is, where are all the customers?

You need to ask yourself a few questions.

- Who's your local competition?
- What do the locals prefer? Bars or restaurants?
- Could outside seating be a problem considering the temperamental UK weather?

- Are the snacks enough to satisfy a big appetite?

- Can anyone actually pronounce the name of your bar?

As you form your answers, it will likely dawn on you that you've not done your homework at all. Yes, your idea was a good one, but:

- What about your location?

- Are you meeting a local need?

- Why aren't there any other bars on the same street?

- Was there really a gap in the market?

- Was it simply the wrong opportunity in the wrong place?

Making the right choice of location has to be one of the major considerations before you dive in with both feet. In the same way that a hog roast probably won't work in the middle of Golders Green, with its predominantly Jewish population, a slick city-style bar won't thrive in a deprived, run-down area. Don't fall into the trap of opening a new venue without first thinking whether there's a disconnect between your proposition and your target customer base. It's vital you cover the basics before signing a lease that probably won't be easy to extract yourself from. It can be an expensive mistake to rectify.

Do your research

I'm constantly amazed how many aspiring entrepreneurs in the hospitality sector don't do their homework. Identifying your customer base, its habits and its unfilled needs is as important a part of the business equation as the passion that drives you to believing you have a great idea for a restaurant or bar. Your next step is to work out:

- Is there a local market for your offering?

- Do your potential customers choose to spend their leisure time in the locality?

- What are their lifestyle choices?

- Do they like to socialise?

- How do they spend their money?

Building a picture of your target demographic will demonstrate if it matches your restaurant or bar. For example, an area populated with late-night kebab shops or takeaways is unlikely to fit a target market made up of prosecco-drinking professionals. As a rule, it's easier to fit in with an existing demographic in an area and introduce new items on to your menu than it is to 'force the entry' in the hope of educating the market or gentrifying the area. Therefore, you need to serve existing demands and tailor your offering to the appetites and interests of the locals.

Be aware of the bigger picture before you make any knee-jerk decisions, taking time to research the local area you're targeting. Once you know your area, a good place to start you research is www.gov.uk to check the legalities and implications of running a hospitality business. The website also provides you with current alcohol licensing in your area at www.gov.uk/alcohol-licence-your-area. Finding empty properties without leaving your chair is easy. Simply visit www.commerciallistings.cbre.co.uk/en-GB/listings/pubsleisure/search or www.intrinsicproperty.co.uk to browse the many in our towns and cities that are crying out for businesses to take up residence. Then dig a little deeper to identify which bars or restaurants are on the market on websites such as www.daviscofferlyons.co.uk, taking some time to examine local footfall via https://brc.org.uk/retail-insight-analytics.

This 'try before you buy' research will offer you valuable insights into where your target market spends its time and money, but there's no substitute for actually getting off your backside and walking the area where you believe your offering will make a difference, talking to the local people. This is the legwork part of the process.

Once you've identified an opportunity, make it your business to find out how good for business it really is. Spend time in the area you've pinpointed morning, noon and night and look closely at how breakfast, lunch and supper times compare. Are the locals really the customers you want to appeal to? Pay careful attention to the style of the street, its décor and architectural designs, and whether it is in a good state of repair. All your observations will go towards creating a powerful portrait of a community with distinctive needs.

In particular, note the following:

- What cars are parked nearby? Flashy and expensive, trade vans or family vehicles?

- What shops are nearby? Bargain basements and charity shops? Barbers or top-end hair design studios?

- After the early school run, do parents drive off and disappear, or do they look like they could be enticed into having something to eat and drink?

- Is car parking freely available and/or accessible nearby?

- How good (or bad) is the nearest public transport service in case your guests have one too many, and how late does it run?

- Does the area die at the weekends, or does it have a life of its own?

Of course, there's no magic formula to opening a successful restaurant, but you'll stand a much better chance of success if you enter into it with your eyes wide open.

Know your neighbours

The saying goes 'birds of a feather flock together', and I believe that's certainly true in the restaurant/bar trade. Although it might seem counterintuitive, your best bet will be to locate your business in an area where it will be surrounded by other bars and restaurants. You'll be in good company with like-minded businesses, even if they are your competitors, because what their presence immediately tells you is that they're making a success in your industry in the locality you want to be in. They'll already have done some of the legwork for you in attracting customers who want to spend money with them.

That's not to suggest your offering needs to be more of the same. In fact, the reverse is true. You need to differentiate yourself in order to stand out from the crowd, but choosing the right location for your customers is the critical first step.

Visibility

In most towns and cities, you'll often find that one side, or one end, of a street is better than the other. You'll most definitely want to avoid the dead spots, even though the leases are cheaper. For bars and restaurants particularly, this is a false economy, because customers can be lazy.

If your venue has little or no visibility because it's tucked around a corner or down the end of an alleyway, your customers won't bother to find you, and you'll be waiting on a lot of empty tables. I realise this may sound obvious, but countless businesses have fallen into the trap of taking a less expensive lease while still expecting customers to be aware of their fabulous restaurant/bar. The truth is, low visibility only adds one more obstacle to your success – one you certainly don't need.

More than anything, your frontage has to be highly visible because it's prime advertising space. Therefore, keep it clear and big. When potential customers drive by, they will need to know what you're offering, or if you're dependent on pedestrian footfall, ensure that your visibility is good not only from both sides of the street, but also from a distance. You may be rightly proud of your hidden gem, but if it's hidden, then it's invisible.

Accessibility

You might have created the most amazing space, but if your customers can't easily drive (and park), walk, or take public transport to it, it's unlikely your distinctive offering will maintain its attraction. The same goes for your employees. Asking them to work anti-social hours and making their homeward journey difficult, unpleasant or tiresome will be a barrier to them, and an impediment to you. Your business will need commitment and passion from your staff, so don't make things hard for them when they leave after a long shift.

There are some restaurants that overcome this obstacle to become *the* destination worth making the effort to get to. However, this will rely on your customers consciously deciding to go that extra mile (literally, or otherwise). From my experience, I'll only visit the 'off the beaten track' places in my area occasionally, especially since I have plenty of other options that serve great food, have good ambience and, crucially, are convenient and easy to get to. And I'm pretty convinced I'm not alone in thinking that way.

Walking in your customers' shoes, ask yourself whether what you're offering is unique enough to merit the effort and commitment needed to spend time and money in your 'off the beaten track' establishment.

Size matters

Small may look beautiful, but do your sums and calculate the number of covers you will need to make a profit. Don't forget, the kitchen, storage facilities and office will all require a reasonable amount of space, and that's before you think about setting out the dining area and bar. Customers don't enjoy sitting at tightly crammed-in tables where they can almost eat from the table next to them and have to endure hearing a loud stranger describe their new house in excruciating detail. Worse still, it's not at all pleasant being enveloped by other people's ~~odour~~... I mean perfume.

I certainly don't return to places that are too intimate. Believe me, I've experienced the scenarios I've just described on many occasions, and while I'm all for maximising revenue, you need to strike the right balance.

Safety

This may not seem immediately obvious, but it's an important consideration for your customers when they're choosing where to spend their money. In particular if you're converting premises under a 'change of use' agreement, it's vital you're aware of current health and safety regulations, and that your staff are adequately trained. Your customers will want to feel safe in the event of an emergency.

Remember that the disabled, the elderly and families with very young children like to go out to eat and drink. Ensure you go beyond the bare minimum and make your place attractive and welcoming to them, too. This will likely involve some capital outlay if you are taking on a site that hasn't been used for hospitality before, because you must ensure that you comply with all the necessary regulations. You can find many of them on this website: www.hse.gov.uk/catering/index.htm.

Lease and commitments

Having identified your venue and carried out your market research, you'll probably have an idea what the going rates for the lease should be. Talk to other business owners in the same area to gauge what you think is a fair price. You'll still have room to negotiate the cost.

My best advice at this stage is not to tie yourself into a long lease that will be a millstone around your neck should the business fail to take off. Sometimes, it pays to be little pessimistic. Leaseholders might have good reasons for charging more for a particular property, but don't be afraid to haggle over the monthly rent. Anything you can shave from their top figure affects your bottom line, especially when you factor in extra costs such as maintenance and waste collections.

The cursed site

Every town has its cursed site. At first glance, the location seems fine; it's on a busy street with a number of successful businesses all doing very well, but for some reason, this one site always seems to fail within months, no matter how hard the tenants try.

If you're not familiar with the area itself, press the landlord for more information as to how many leases have come and gone on the property, and how long each tenant stayed. If you don't get a straight answer, do some more homework. The best place to start is to talk to local residents or shop owners who often unearth a wealth of hidden clues you'll not find anywhere else. For example, the site might carry a poor reputation from previous restaurants for substandard food or lack of ambience. Both of these are factors that can deter potential customers over which you'll have no control.

If all the previous tenants have failed to make their businesses work in a particular property, this is a red flag, even if you're convinced you can make a go of it. However, it could be that your offering will buck the trend, so despite all the warning signs, if you still want to give it a go, mitigate the risks with a short-term lease.

Defining and styling your concept

With much of your homework in the bag, you're ready to map out your plan to build and manage your business. On the whole, this is how the restaurant industry works, so it's as well not to deviate from it.

What makes a good concept? Everything from the food to the interior design and location of the venue. This then feeds into your customer demographic and overall pricing structure.

The most important place to start is with *you*. What style of food inspires you and defines you as a chef or entrepreneur? Draw on your own heritage, your upbringing and travel experiences, and places you've eaten in that have inspired you. The tricky part is deciding on which aspect speaks to you most since you'll be pulled in numerous conflicting directions. For example, your interior design preference might not necessarily match your food proposition, or your intended price point.

On a positive note, introducing a fusion or twist might give you a competitive edge – a unique spin attractive to customers looking for something a little different in the area where they currently eat or drink. In fact, restaurants that offer something unique stand a much better chance of survival. However, remember to match your passion with the demographic where your bar or restaurant will be located. Unless you've carried out thorough market research, your great concept may be ruined through lack of planning. Essentially you need to be clear about what your concept is and what it stands for, and then make sure you stick to it.

The figure below shows the different service offerings. It's important that the one you select directly relates to your restaurant concept because it will inform the diner's overall experience. Spend some time considering what your service offering will be, so that when you open, you are properly managing your customers' expectations. For example, it would be difficult to match fine-dining service with burgers.

You may be surprised how many restaurant owners confuse their service style with their concept, and thereby confuse their customers. Your restaurant might be an absolutely fabulous bistro, but if you describe yourself as 'fine dining', you'll be heading down a misleading path.

However, more and more, the lines between service styles are becoming blurred, and hybrids are emerging in response to customers' changing demands and habits. For example, 'fine-casual' (credited to Shake Shack founder Danny Meyer) is a rapidly rising trend in the bigger metropolitan centres, speaking to the heart of the time-poor customer seeking something a little out of the ordinary. These eateries meld the speed and convenience of fast-casual with a chef-driven menu on which you wouldn't be surprised to find lobster served in a burger bun. Increasingly, the restaurant business is a fluid marketplace that often reinvents itself, feeding consumers' cravings for new cuisines and experiences while accommodating their demand for speed and convenience.

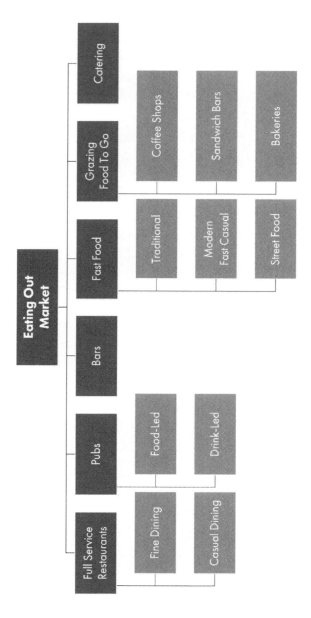

Figure 3.1 Service offerings

Determining your food and drink proposition

Let's assume that you've settled on your location, which is neatly placed in the heart of your target customers' leisure activities, and gained clarity on your concept. Now's the time to finalise the details of the food and drink you will be serving to tie your concept together.

Your research will have given you an idea of what food and drink could work best on your menu, and this will allow you some room for experimentation. However, be warned: customers like to think they're more adventurous than they really are when it comes to trying out new dishes. If you're tempted to build your reputation on speciality offal dishes, I'd advise you to include one or two safer options to cater for your more squeamish guests. If your service style is a French bistro, it wouldn't make sense to include a fusion dish of tapas and sushi, since this wouldn't meet your diners' expectations.

Follow your gut feeling and adopt a sensible approach that won't alienate any diners. Your reputation will be founded on your creative award-winning dishes, while your safer options will still reflect your concept, perhaps with a unique twist that sets you apart without confusing your customers. You'll never be able to cater for all tastes, but as a general rule, the smaller the menu, the better. Who wants to wade through page upon page of menu items that suggest the food can't possibly be fresh and prepared to order? Your customers are more discerning than that, and given the choice, they'll prefer a carefully designed menu with just enough variety.

'Fresh' is a big motivator when customers are looking to spend money in your restaurant. We can all cook ready meals at home, so include and signpost as many freshly cooked dishes as possible.

Customers are also increasingly attracted to 'local'. They'll love the fact that your meat, eggs, vegetables, even beers and juices have been sourced locally. Flagging these as your standards and values says so much about you and your business. Your pride in supporting local suppliers will help differentiate your venue from others, demonstrating your commitment to contributing to the local economy in meaningful ways. If you can add support for ethical production and high welfare standards, then you are on to a winner.

The quality of your ingredients is key to your business's success, reputation and profitability. High-cost items can make a real difference, but there will always be less expensive alternatives that don't compromise on taste or quality. Knowing your food, its origins, and how various combinations can add to, or detract from, flavour sensations will give you an upper hand in working out how to cost your menus.

It's also vital you avoid too much waste by understanding how the same ingredients can be used in different dishes such as a sauce or dip. Truffles are a good example of this: expensive as a single item on a dish, but equally tasty in a sauce that won't need the customer to take out a mortgage.

If you don't know how many servings you can make from a side of salmon, for example, then make finding out a top priority. Learn how to use the whole fish, bones included, to create soups and sauces. As your business develops, regularly monitor what sells and what doesn't, and always include a combination of high- and low-cost items. Refresh your menu on a regular basis with new items and be ruthless in removing dishes that struggle to sell.

I'm often asked what happens when a guest wants their meal customised to suit a certain taste. My advice is to give them what they want, as long as the dish still resembles what's on the menu and remains acceptable from an aesthetic and cost perspective. Research shows we are all hardwired with the desire to choose, and in satisfying this desire, we become fulfilled and happy. Customisation is a powerful tool that taps into this innate desire since it empowers consumers through choices.

We can't control everything in our lives, but we can control what we put into our bodies. Customers really appreciate any effort you make to accommodate their tastes and treat them like the individuals they are, and these customers will reward tailored dining with repeat business and higher spend.

At one time, vegetarian and vegan options weren't featured on a menu, beyond the mandatory stuffed mushrooms. These days, though, they should be offered as standard. How satisfying is it when a carnivore customer willingly chooses a vegetarian option over the steak just because it sounds so tempting and tasty on the menu? Show customers that you care about their dietary preferences and cater for them.

State your policy on allergens, particularly nuts, as clearly as clear can be. I'm sure I don't need to tell you how dangerous these can be if ingested by someone who has a severe allergy. Think carefully whether you wish to make your restaurant entirely nut-free, or include them while clearly showing which dishes contain them. Train your staff, empowering them with knowledge about your menu and how dishes are prepared. If they're not able to tell the customers in great detail what each dish contains, then how will your customers make an informed decision?

Alcohol always used to be a dependable way to make a tidy profit, but customers' drinking habits are changing. It's said that in the UK, one in five people now describes themselves as teetotal, increasing to one in three in London. This is bad news if you're depending on making a meaningful mark-up by selling a lot of alcohol. Obviously, your drinks menu will depend on your business and clientele, but you may well need to pay greater attention to your alcohol-free selection. It should be wide and appealing enough for customers to choose something other than tap water, where you make no margin at all.

Finally, steer clear of the latest fads. Anything that is likely to be gimmicky simply won't be sustainable. Before you know it, another fad will have replaced the last one, and you'll forever be playing catch up. This isn't to say you can't innovate from time to time, but it doesn't have to be a full-on revolution.

Choosing your brand name

The name above your door should give your customers a pretty good idea of the type of food you serve. My top tips are:

- Keep it short and simple

- Make it memorable

- Be authentic

- Avoid anything too crazy

- Make sure no other venue is using the same or a similar name. Beware trademark infringement by checking here: https://trademarks.ipo.gov.uk/ipo-tmtext

Basically, don't let your brand name make your life difficult, and in particular, don't make it hard for your customers and suppliers to remember. For example, if you're considering changing the spelling of a familiar word or phrase to create a new twist, bear in mind you'll have to spell it out each time suppliers need to write it down.

How to approach creating a brand name is open to all sorts of interpretations, but quite often, owners take inspiration from their location, a signature dish, or even a family member who inspires them. Once you've decided on a few options, run them by people outside of your immediate circle so you can receive honest feedback. Are they getting what your brand really stands for from the names you've chosen? If not, then think again. Be curious and inquisitive all the time, ready to take positive and negative criticism on board in all aspects of your business.

Also, think about your aspirations for future growth. Are you intending to scale up and expand? Perhaps your brand will go global, so use a word or phrase that can be easily pronounced in other languages. If you think your food offering might change in the future, don't include it as part of the name.

At the top of this chapter, I advised you 'to thine own self be true'. I'll now add 'get it right first time', and that definitely applies to the name of your brand. Your brand name is a worthy advertising asset because of the impression it creates about you and your offering. Therefore, it's worth taking the time to be completely confident in your name before you pick up the paintbrush or print your menus.

Inspiration

Your wish to create a venue that stands out from the rest might result in some sleepless nights. How far can you go? Will customers beat a path to your door?

The good news is that in the UK, a wide variety of dining options are opening up. From high end to cafés and street food vans, owners are daring to be different and thriving on their growing reputations for innovation, creativity and the ability to offer their customers a unique experience.

Some of my favourite innovative venues include:

- The Library Restaurant, Norwich – housed in the UK's first subscription library with a theme to match, this restaurant serves up tasty dishes cooked to order under wood-fired grills

- The Attendant, London – a converted Victorian public toilet, now a trendy café. It almost sounds counterintuitive as a location for a food offering, but its distinct quirkiness has proved to be a successful draw for hungry customers

- Death Row Dive and Diner, Liverpool – if you were about to have your last meal, you'd want it to be a good one. With its minimalist décor and gruesome sense of humour, this unique venue reminds diners that life really is wonderful

- Cereal Killer Café, London – as the name suggests, the venue specialises in breakfast favourites with an added twist, including flavoured milks to suit all tastes

- The Clink, Cardiff – this charity led concept employs ex-offenders to learn new skills as they re-enter society. To serve bad food would be criminal, so The Clink makes every effort to create mouth-watering dishes

- Frying Nemo, Goole – since its introduction to the UK by refugee Jews, fish and chips has become one of the country's staples. And there's no better place to eat them than beside the sea, where competition can be fierce. A name that stands out is a huge advantage

Your staff

There are many boxes you need to tick before you can even think about revealing your concept and brand to the wider world. Having gone through all the checks, can you confidently say you have the right tools to deliver your concept? Specifically, do you have the right staff? Are they as impassioned and knowledgeable as you are about your offering? If not, they need to be on message so that they can deliver a truly bespoke experience for every customer who walks through the door.

Over the years, working in many areas of hospitality, I've seen what it's like to be running a business as well as working in one, so trust me when I say that your staff can make or break your idea. They should be your greatest asset, so in the next chapter I'll share my practical advice to help them help you transform your restaurant and realise your vision.

CHAPTER FOUR

Tailoring Your Brand Experience Through Your People

In the previous chapter, we discussed the various key elements you need to pull together to make the vision of your dream restaurant become a reality. Research, homework and due diligence aside, though, once you're ready to cut the ribbon, the success of your venture will rest heavily on how well you invest in your staff.

You'll not achieve success on your own. You might be the best multi-tasker you know, but in the hectic world of hospitality, you can't be in all places all of the time. Your staff will be your front line ambassadors, so it's vital that you think carefully about the skills you need them to bring to the table and, more importantly, the personalities that will help your brand experience succeed.

Serving great food won't be enough, so it's up to you to pay special attention to the people you employ. Make sure they are fully engaged with your brand, its service and offering, so that they, too, are empowered to bring it to life.

In this chapter, I'll be discussing how to hire the right staff. By carefully aligning your staff to your brand, you'll not only make a direct connection between you and your customers, you'll also create enhanced, tailored experiences that will set you apart and encourage repeat business.

Career vs it's just a job

Attitudes towards hiring people to staff bars and restaurants are slowly changing in the UK, but the pace needs to pick up. In France, for example, working in a bar or restaurant is regarded as more of a career choice than a job that requires little or no commitment.

'At first we were for the lowly servants of society. If you were an economic failure or had a frontal lobotomy, you automatically came into hospitality.'
—Raymond Blanc in an article for *The Caterer*, May 2018

While Blanc's view is laced with a *soupçon* of humour, there is an underlying truth in what he says. If we don't attract good people into the industry and provide them with real and meaningful training, then the cycle of restaurant failures will repeat itself, and that's not good for brands, the hospitality sector, or the paying customers.

Training our biggest assets in hospitality has to step up several gears in order to keep up with changing customer expectations and needs. It should no longer be limited to handing out a staff manual and taking the dreaded health and safety courses; it needs to encompass the brand, its values and what it stands for fully. This is complete alignment in practice, and it's beginning to gain significance and popularity, not just from the employer's perspective, but for the employees, too.

Studies reveal that better trained hospitality staff are not only more enthusiastic about their work, they are also much better at promoting the brand and its values to the customers, which leads to a significantly higher return on tips. Ultimately, you want your team to live and breathe your brand because they are on the front line, representing everything you stand for. Enthusiasm is contagious, but so is gloom. After all, nobody enjoys being greeted by a glum server with little or no knowledge of what's available or the story behind it.

If you're completely driven by your concept, your people should be too, and the fit needs to be seamless. For example, a vibrant cocktail bar which is packed at weekends with guests celebrating good times needs a team that's vivacious and outgoing. However, that team would be entirely out of place in a more reserved fine-dining environment. This may seem obvious, but I've certainly been to places where the staff can't help but ruin my experience. Who wants to spend their money when they're greeted by staff who lack positive engagement or personality?

Studies have shown that over a third of customers won't return to a venue after one bad experience, and this of course impacts negatively on the business. The question is, who's responsible? In my opinion, it's almost always the brand owner, which is why I am on a mission to remind bar and restaurant owners that proper staff training needs to be a high priority. It can be all too easily overlooked when anti-social hours and pressured environments mean that time runs away, but good training practice within the workplace culture will raise industry-wide standards from the very outset, and you will reap the rewards once your brand is on a roll.

Attracting staff

Use your judgement wisely. In the same way that you carried out detailed research for your concept, the same goes for recruiting your people. Don't be afraid to look beyond the typical recruit if you feel your brand is calling out for someone different. We need to move away from the stereotypical candidate of Raymond Blanc's observation. For example, in a family restaurant, a college leaver or student looking to bolster their loan will not necessarily have the same skills and intuition as a parent when it comes to dealing with a stressed-out mum and her hyperactive child.

This 360-degree thinking is backed up by industry research which shows that employers, especially in the service industries, recognise that their staff make a significant impact on the overall guest experience. This, in turn, translates into increased customer spending levels in excess of 15%, which just goes to show the importance of creating a positive experience for your customers.

To achieve that experience, you as a business owner need to lead from the front. It's your responsibility to lead your employees by example when you're interacting with guests. Invest time and energy 'on the floor', away from the day-to-day back-office work. It will offer you the greatest insights from the ground up, since you'll see first hand where your team needs additional help to deliver the bespoke services your guests want.

Your staff will also learn valuable lessons from you on how to engage with customers, especially the unreasonable and awkward ones. Aligning your team to your business vision through a direct and personable approach will encourage them to rise to the challenge of delivering service in a way that fits your concept. As a result, they'll feel encouraged to feed back to you on what's working well and what needs improvement.

When I was young, one of my favourite stories revolved around a character called 'Mrs-Do-As-You-Would-Be-Done-By', and her attitude is exactly what you need when you're working with your team. Yes, you must show firm leadership, but soft skills are equally important. Encourage your staff to give their best in return for being treated as you and your guests would like to be treated.

For example, if you run a restaurant, offer your team the same food, for free, that you serve on your menu. Otherwise, how can you expect them to connect positively with the restaurant or speak knowledgeably and authentically when they're describing the dishes to your customers? If your staff love your food, they'll certainly tell your customers, and they'll be incentivised further to remain working with you, not just because the food is a free perk of the job, but because it *is* the job.

It may take time and money to invest in your staff and their training, but if your mission includes creating a good experience for them as well as your customers, your staff turnover rate will drop dramatically. Just as a high percentage of customers won't return after a bad experience, the same applies to your staff. An unhappy, poorly trained, often-criticised and demotivated staff member can wreak havoc with absenteeism, low morale and bad service. Immerse them in your vision and your brand, and they will take pleasure in sharing their experiences of your food, while your customers will appreciate the staff's complete commitment to it.

Not investing in your people simply isn't a sensible strategy, especially if you have invested heavily in every other area of your business.

Employee expectations

Without doubt, the make-up of the workforce is continually evolving. Leading recruitment agency Manpower's 'Millennial Careers: 2020 Vision' report (2016) shows that by 2020, 35% of the workforce will be made up of Millennials. Millennials are more used to challenging each other and working together in order to find the best creative solutions to problems than previous generations, aided by their familiarity with technology.

From an employer's standpoint, they need to understand and embrace the Millennials' priorities. Research by Fidelity Investments (July 2016) shows that Millennials are prepared to accept up to £5,700 less pay per annum in return for a balanced lifestyle. Therefore, when Millennials say they care about flexibility and openness, you need to step up to their plate (and not the other way round) if you want to motivate your staff. James Hacon believes it is time to apply 'a little creativity – or a lot of flexibility'.

Helping your staff feel happy, confident and motivated is key to maintaining your brand's high standards. If you embrace the changing nature of staff expectations, lifestyles and habits, you will encourage everyone in the business to contribute towards its success.

- Consider your working hours – could a four-day working week keep staff motivated and energy levels up? Could staff who want to go travelling have their job kept open for their return?

- Offer your staff a stake in the company with share options or a bonus scheme to encourage a sense of ownership

- Enable staff to be mini entrepreneurs by asking them to think of ways in which the business could be improved or allowing them to take real leadership over certain functions

- Solicit their thoughts and ideas on marketing your brand, taking advantage of their social media skills

- Nominate them for industry awards (mixology, best sommelier, best marketer, young chefs) in order to stimulate innovation and creative thinking

- Establish your own company-wide award schemes that recognise best practice and achievements

- Empower staff to solve disgruntled customer problems without pre-authorisation using small but meaningful gestures such as upgrades, a free drink or a discount

- Encourage professional development in other aspects of the business to stimulate skills

- Engage team members in the choice of a charity scheme that fits your brand to encourage a sense of ownership

- Facilitate offsite voluntary work during work hours without penalty

- Schedule regular and frequent feedback instead of the dreaded annual review

- Don't assume that your team members want to participate in an outward-bound activity day – instead, ask them what they would like to try as a team-bonding exercise

- Recognise each team member's individuality

- Provide staff with food and beverages that you serve to customers

Any one, or all, of these initiatives is invaluable in terms of recognition not only for your individual staff members, but also for your brand. If you worry that you might lose talented staff members to your competition, it's worth investing the effort and taking risks to guide and inspire them. I'm sure you know from your own experiences that a large part of your decision to return to certain bars and restaurants is based on the people who make them memorable and worthwhile.

THE EXPERT'S OPINION
– ANDRE MANNINI –

M restaurants have been leading the way within the hospitality industry by ensuring that they not only look after their people, but also improve their staff's mental health and well-being.

Clearly, working in hospitality, with its long hours and demanding roles, is tough, and for too long the problems it creates have been ignored or simply regarded as 'rites of passage'. The chef as a 'bully', ruling his (and yes, generally it is 'his') kitchen, is a well-known and even celebrated figure. But a growing realisation, led by, but not exclusive to, the Millennial generation, is resulting in a call for better conditions and more flexible working.

I developed a number of initiatives to combat the problem of mental stress and overworking. For example, M-indful days are (paid) days given to employees to use how they wish. They could be used simply to rest/recover or for an out-of-work interest/ hobby. This negates the need for staff to 'pull a sickie' and incentivises good planning and more responsible and mature behaviour. These M-indful days are added to the staff member's holiday allowance, or the staff member is paid at the end of the year if they don't use the days. This initiative has been incredibly well received by the staff and management, and now other restaurants are taking note.

M restaurants also encourage 'sabbaticals' for managers who have achieved staff retention targets and great staff survey results. These paid days off are added to the manager's annual holiday allowance, elongating their annual leave to make it a proper switch off from work.

Mental health is enhanced by the availability of counselling, where staff can talk to someone before they need to talk to someone. This counselling uses technology combined with professional help and confidentiality, enabling M's people to be fully supported in their challenging roles.

The development of skills is a key factor in motivating M restaurants' people and encouraging them to stay. I can now point to staff who have been mentored and given the opportunities to move into other roles within the business. There is no reason why one of our talented waiting staff will not one day be our financial director.

Through creating bespoke roles and jobs, we are able to train our people in different areas to give them new opportunities and challenges, meaning they actively want to stay with us.

**Andre Mannini is Operations Director
of M Restaurants.**

Part Two

CHAPTER FIVE

Understanding Choice

Let's be honest: in the main, the hospitality industry has fallen behind other industries that have adopted customisation as a tool to attract and retain their customers.

The time of producing standardised products on a mass scale is over as the market changes along with customer demands and expectations. We see it from the luxury car market to personalised monogrammed handbags. You may think this bears no relation to the steak burgers you serve or the cocktails you shake – after all, your customers are probably not the likes of Roman Abramovich or Kim Kardashian who can well afford luxury customisation to the nth degree. But that doesn't mean to say your customers don't share similar aspirations to have things served their way.

Understanding how the customer psyche is changing, what triggers their choices and how they respond to your offering is a key element that the hospitality industry needs to embrace, from the corner café to the fine-dining establishment. Customisation has arrived, and combined with the experience economy, it will have a major impact on how successful your business will be, and how it can remain competitive in a marketplace where choice is uppermost.

For example, when there were only five terrestrial TV channels to choose from, we watched programmes broadcast to the masses. When the disruptors arrived on the scene – Netflix and Amazon Prime video – customer demands and habits changed, so much so that the traditional broadcasters had to follow suit and develop their own streaming services in order to remain alive and competitive.

In hospitality, we can see how quickly casual outlets such as Five Guys or Subway disrupted the industry by offering consumers a vast array of choices to have things their own way. And this trend is filtering upwards as customers become accustomed to having greater choices over what they eat. They want to be co-creating with you to be a part of the experience, because it gives them a sense of satisfaction when they have something that is uniquely theirs.

Throughout Part Two, therefore, I will be guiding you through a mixed menu of customisation elements that the hospitality industry needs to adopt/adapt so that you can meet your customers' demands and continue to grow.

How psychology influences choice

In his book *The Paradox of Choice*, Dr Barry Schwartz divides consumers into two groups based on their decision-making habits:

- 'Maximisers' are perfectionists who agonise over making choices and need to explore each option in great detail before they decide – even if the first option they consider is perfect

- 'Satisficers' make a decision or take action once their basic criteria are met

There's no one-size-fits-all approach to anything in life, so it's important that restaurants and bars cater to both types by offering straightforward, pragmatic information that includes detailed, appealing descriptions.

Psychologists generally agree that when people have choices, they feel more in control. Leading psychologist Professor Sheena Iyengar, who specialises in understanding why and how humans make the choices they do, tells us that the ability to make choices is 'essential for an individual's well-being'. She states that choice is not only the perceived extension of feeling in control, it's also a biological necessity. Restricting people's opportunities to choose creates an adverse environment that impacts negatively upon our inner psyche, which has its roots in our need for survival. In short, being able to choose makes us feel happy, which then translates into the power of decision making.

If you apply this simple yet powerful psychological concept to a menu, which by its nature facilitates the ability to choose, it's possible to empower diners by encouraging them to take action. On a menu, choices need to be clearly indicated within a comparative context so the diner can assess their options and make their choices based on their own preferences.

For example, if a diner selects dishes that are advertised as sharing platters, this information motivates their choice and helps feed their unconscious desire to feel in control of their spending. Your menu can direct them towards items you want to promote while remaining within the context of the customer having the power to choose. However, beware of offering too much choice since this may overload your customer's brain, resulting in poor decision making that leaves them confused and dissatisfied.

Consumer choice is also influenced by personalisation. Car manufacturers have long since recognised that buyers base their purchasing decisions on more and more complex criteria, from exterior car colour to interior features and technological specs. It's my firm belief that personalisation is set to hit the hospitality industry like a ten-tonne truck. It's vital, therefore, that we know how to embrace it so that our customers are as engaged as anyone purchasing a car. This might include offering different portion sizes, sides instead of mains, or substituting certain ingredients.

I'm not alone in this thinking. Beth Johnson, Executive Director of Special Projects for personalised digital media company, Catalina, notes that 'personalisation and shopper choice are not just about savings, [they're] also about communicating to consumers in the manner in which they prefer'.

Choice is much more complex than simply listing what food and drink you're offering. My contention is that if you can gain a deeper understanding of the psychology that lies behind your customers' decision-making process, it'll then be possible to target them more effectively by appealing to their own sense of individuality while maximising your potential profits.

Let your menu do the talking

Your menu is your only advertising point that 100% of paying customers will study for up to two minutes with the sole intent to purchase – this is almost unheard of these days in marketing terms. When did you last see a TV ad that ran for two minutes? Your menu is an important opportunity for your customers to digest what it is you're advertising, most probably online in the first instance while their appetite is whetted, followed by sitting at a table with it in their hands.

It doesn't matter whether you run a small café or a fine-dining establishment, how your menu looks and feels is reflective of both you and your brand. From the outset, it plays a crucial role in communicating your personality, standards and beliefs accurately. It must also meet your customers' taste preferences and culinary desires. It tells them if you're ethical or pretentious, if you're well-travelled and adventurous, or if you're local community focused. All these nuggets of information, therefore, need to be reflected in the menu and how you word it.

Do restaurants and bars get their menus wrong? Absolutely! Not all, of course, but many make the same common mistakes. I want to help you understand the psychology of diners so you can recalibrate your approach to menu design and planning in response, selecting the elements you can improve upon and implementing customisation to satisfy your guests.

Expect to excite customers so much that they'll still be talking about your offering and recommending it to their friends and families long after their visit. Once it's placed in their hands, your menu directly influences not only what they will order, but ultimately how much they will spend.

In the following sections, I'll show how you maximise the opportunity your menu presents to return the greatest profit while keeping your price points within the customers' expectations. To achieve this, you first need to understand that the five main goals of a well-designed menu are to:

- Act as an effective communication, marketing and cost-control tool

- Emphasise what the customer wants that matches what the restaurant/bar prepares and serves best

- Achieve the required minimum average spend per head to realise sales goals and bottom-line return

- Utilise staff and equipment in an efficient manner

- Forecast the future menu sales mix more accurately

Steps to take before planning and designing a menu

Think of this stage in 360 degrees. No single vision will achieve a menu that hits all the right notes. To be clear and effective, it has to be a team decision from the owner and representatives of management, chef and customer focus groups. Reading and responding to feedback should be one of the first steps you undertake in designing a menu.

A survey conducted by Gallup revealed that customers will spend an average of 109 seconds reading the menu. If it reads like a culinary novella, it isn't necessarily going to have a happy ending. I'll explain what this means in financial terms later on.

An article posted by the blogsite HubSpot stated that choice is 'the purest expression of free will – the freedom to choose allows us to shape our lives exactly how we wish'. This struck home for me. Having worked in and analysed the hospitality industry over many years, I've regularly seen frustrated looks on customers' faces when they're confronted with either too much or too little choice. Too few options feels restrictive, uncreative and unfulfilling, whereas a long list of dishes is overwhelming, and both scenarios often end negatively, with the customer either leaving or having a less-than-exemplary experience.

This is why I firmly believe that understanding the psychology of choice is one of the most important things anyone running a hospitality business can do. It's vitally important that you make the most of the opportunity to engage your customer from the second they look at your menu. Time is on your side since the customer will spend an average of 109 seconds looking at the menu, thinking and discussing what you're offering with their fellow diners. At this moment, your diners are a captive audience, so grab them while they're excited and eager to spend their money.

For example, TGI Friday initially introduced a twelve-page menu which included so many items, it was overwhelming and made decision-making more confusing. The group has since reduced its menu to four pages.

Although a variety of choices is integral for every restaurant or bar, too many owners believe that the bigger the choice, the better. That's not what I mean by customisation at all; that's simply overloading the customer with too much information to process, as well as fuelling their suspicion that the dishes are not either individually or freshly prepared.

Sheena Iyengar in her TED talk 'How to Make Choosing Easier' refers to a study she conducted at a grocery store in Palo Alto, USA. In a controlled experiment, she discovered that patrons were 33% less likely to stop and sample from a display of six varieties of jam, as opposed to another display of twenty-four varieties. However, the surprise finding was that more customers converted their sampling into actual sales from the display of six varieties. Put simply, when faced with the 'paradox of choice' (as defined by the Harvard Business Review), the customer will spend less.

Of course, diversity of choice is a different matter altogether, but a detrimental overload isn't the answer. This fact is borne out by research from Mental Floss, a digital, print and e-commerce media company that focuses on Millennials. Its analysis claims that the 'golden number' is seven options per food category: seven appetiser, seven main course and seven dessert options. In my opinion, this is a sensible way forward.

As a rule, then, when you're planning and designing your menu, bear the following in mind:

- Cut choices to avoid overwhelming consumers
- Be honest
- Categorise choices to make items easier to find
- Be prepared to offer customisation

These are staple requirements of any menu and will remain essential for the foreseeable future.

How consumers choose items from your menu

Let's catch up with Dan and Zoë. As soon as Dan sits down at the table, he's immediately aware of the enticing smell of grilled steak in the air, and even before he looks at the menu, he's made up his mind that he wants to order something that tastes as good as it smells. When he opens the slim but stylish menu, his eyes are drawn straight to the highlighted house specialities, and something catches his eye: the steak tartare. He's fascinated by the descriptions of 'organically hand-reared Norfolk beef' and 'silky raw egg yolk with a brash hit of citrus', which appeals to his health-conscious appetite and gym-toned body.

It's going to be an easy decision for Dan, even though steak tartare isn't the cheapest option on offer. After all, tonight's a special night – his girlfriend's birthday – and he's feeling adventurous. Zoë's impressed with his choice and also decides to try the steak tartare – it's a new dish for both of them and they can't wait to taste it.

The choices we make as individuals are not only reflections of our wants and needs, but also our personalities and values. Even when choices are difficult to make, we create the attitudes informing them quickly as we tend to anchor our decisions based around the first piece of information we receive. Our subconscious will react to primers that pique our interest before we arrive at any conscious decision.

This isn't a response we can control, but the primers that stimulate the response can be deliberately triggered. For example, if we walk into a restaurant and there's a wonderful aroma of steak in the air, this might influence us to order it. Or we might catch the smell of freshly baked pastries from a bakery on our way to a restaurant which gives us a desire to have a tasty, sweet dessert at the end of our meal. Primers, from aromas to sounds and colours, exist all around us, and restaurants regularly use them to inform what choices their customers arrive at. Perhaps the strawberry panna cotta will sell particularly well on the night the staff are wearing red ties.

The study of choices and how we make them in restaurants and bars is an area of increasing interest. Research shows that consumers are subconsciously influenced in their decision making through the use of words and phrases that describe colour, taste and aroma. While the more familiar 'Daily Specials' board has a certain pull, complex descriptions which use buzzwords such as 'hand-reared' or 'caramelised' can increase demand by up to 30%, and can also attract a premium.

Professor Dan Jurafsky, a specialist in computational linguistics from California's Stanford University, analysed 650,000 dishes across 6,500 restaurant menus, from Michelin-starred establishments to roadside diners. He discovered that a premium could equate to an extra 18 cents/letter when dishes were described using certain words. Typically, more expensively priced menus that emphasised the food's provenance would use longer words, while cheaper menus employed more basic descriptors such as 'tasty'.

Choice is so deeply influenced by language that in her research into consumer psychology, Sheena Iyengar conducted a study to determine just how powerful naming could be. She presented participants with two bottles of nail polish and asked them to choose which shade they preferred. Most study participants chose a shade named 'Adorable' when presented with label-free bottles. However, when the women knew the names of the polish, the majority chose the opposite shade, named 'Ballet Slippers'. Something as simple as a name completely changed the consumers' choice.

Clearly, then, choosing the perfect names for the items on your menu is essential, with language being as important as the food in enticing your customers to spend more. However, getting the balance right is a fine line as most customers will have a natural aversion to choosing the most expensive items on the menu. Understanding the psychology of pricing and how it relates to the way in which your items are listed is a clever way of driving customers to selecting the dishes that are the most profitable, but not necessarily the most expensive.

Smart pricing

Research carried out by William Poundstone for *Wired Magazine (April 2017), entitled 'The Hidden Psychology of Menu Design',* noted that customers like to fall between the two extremes of the most expensive item at the top of the menu and the cheapest at the bottom. This might seem like an obvious finding, but the lessons behind his study are worth noting. He unpicks the clever tricks of menu design that encourage diners to spend more, for example, the second most expensive wine on the list usually being the most popular consumer choice (and the most profitable).

Poundstone further concluded that:

- Items placed directly below the top (most expensive) item automatically seem like a better deal

- Items displayed in boxes are the most profitable

- Dishes priced for two often appeal to couples who won't be as cost conscious when sharing

- Half portions or deals encourage diners to order more than they would normally because the price points are attractive. Half portions also contain fewer calories

- Prices that are justified to the right-hand side of the page encourage customers to locate the cheapest items easily, whereas centring them on the page encourages the diner to choose what they want, as opposed to making a decision based on cost

One psychological trick that stimulates a customer's unconscious bias is loss aversion. The simple principle is that people don't like to miss out on an item that is available only for a limited time. Describing items as exclusive on a menu makes them more appealing. This explains the fact that 'limited time only' offers consistently succeed in encouraging consumers to make purchases at a higher rate than they would otherwise. Even when bias is clear, its allure cannot always be resisted.

Tapping into the emotions

To add further complexity, diners are not only influenced by the descriptions, placings and costs of the dishes on your menu, they'll sometimes make decisions based on who's with them. According to the *Journal of Consumer Psychology,* people feel 'closer to, and more trusting of, those who consume as they do'.

The lesson here is that customers will often share a dish (especially on a first date) since it demonstrates an affinity. From a business perspective, menu items that appeal to this sensibility are likely to be highly popular, since sharing options engage consumers and motivate choice.

If the location, ambience, price sensitivities etc of your establishment appeal to couples on first dates, understand that your customers are looking for more out of the experience than simply dining with their date. It's not only a functional occasional, it's also a subconscious information gathering exercise. This understanding will determine whether you offer a fitting range of sharing options on the menu.

Also, remember that a restaurant or bar doesn't only appeal to the taste buds or the eyes through its design. We are sentient beings, so sounds, too, can play an important role by evoking nostalgia, which can connect dishes to certain time periods. For example, if you're offering more traditional, 'homely' style dishes, customers like to hear comforting music that reminds them of their early life.

The psychology of listening to music connects with the dining experience in fascinating ways. Music has its upside and downside, in my opinion, and needs careful planning so that it reflects the experience you want to create. If all you care about is making a fast profit, then playing loud music with a fast tempo may make your diners eat more quickly, but research shows that they enjoy their meal less, and drink and eat less, too.

What loud music does is tap into the reptilian brain that encourages 'fight or flight' responses and doesn't leave much time for eating (or enjoying the experience). The opposite, soft and mellow music, helps customers relax and they'll enjoy their food more. They may even experience new taste sensations as a result, where high notes are associated with sweet flavours and low notes associated with bitter tastes.

You need to consider the soundscape of your venue carefully.

Adapting choice to future trends

Methods of influencing consumer choice are forever changing. Whereas at one time, a diner might have asked another at their table for advice on a certain dish, today, it's more likely to be their smartphone.

Instant feedback and connections allow anybody to read shared digital information, with a smiley face here, or a thumbs down there.

For the customer, the upside of this is that it can help them reach a decision more easily and quickly. In the hospitality industry, we need to embrace this trend and incorporate it into our own digital output. If a tasty looking picture is featured alongside a description of a dish in a printed menu, then it should also appear online and be rendered fit for smartphone technology. Research by online media agency, The Hustle, shows that dining establishments adopting this practice have already seen an increase in uptake of as much as 30%. It not only allows you to push certain products, but encourages more visitors to your establishment in the first place.

Whether it's simply mind games or not, the psychology that underpins customers' decision making tells us that wining and dining is perhaps more of a sophisticated industry than we first imagined. From pretentious high-end restaurants to the tattiest café, I firmly believe that psychology can – and does – offer tools to reinvigorate our industry. For too long, we have ignored consumer trends and changing demographic spending habits. Understanding the customer better has to be a good thing if we want to see a thriving hospitality industry in our towns and cities.

Choice is undeniably a complex psychological process, but it's not one you need to be intimidated by. With a little knowledge, you can harness the elements that influence your customers' dining and drinking decisions to improve both their experience and your business performance.

CHAPTER SIX

Customisation

Customisation has arrived in the restaurant and bar industry, and it looks like it's here to stay. Customers are increasingly taking control of what they consume as they analyse menus in great detail, seeking clarity of ingredients and what they mean in terms of calorie and sugar intake.

In 2018, according to MCA, the UK's leading provider of eating and drinking out market intelligence, over 30% of consumers customised their last meal out, while 55% believed that customisation is an essential element when it comes to making their choice. No matter what's included on the menu, it seems that a growing number of consumers want to pick and choose, because that fits their belief that they, not the proprietor, know what suits them best. It's no longer in their nature to compromise on tastes, values or beliefs. What was once considered a passive activity is fast becoming a collaborative effort, with the consumer having the upper hand.

Responding to the trend in consumer habits is one of the biggest challenges that traditional bar and restaurant owners face in order to remain competitive and attract repeat custom. Overwhelming as this might sound, if you implement the right changes, you will be proving that your business is paying close attention to the specific needs of the consumer. The demand for original, specialised and personal choices is a trend which has been hurting even mega brands such as Starbucks, Subway and Chipotle, so you can take some heart in knowing that you're not alone.

Influencing this trend is the proliferation of information and consumer feedback on social media platforms. This has significantly swayed consumers' opinions and helped define their beliefs when it comes to what they eat and drink. The good news is that the hospitality business has always been a reactive one, be it catering to diet fads, serving up popular ingredients and cooking techniques, or plating food on the latest fashion in slate or board. However, what it's unlikely to acknowledge is that the consumer's relationship with restaurant food is increasingly descending into love/hate.

At the turn of the century, the British usually accepted whatever was listed on the menu. No one wanted to be the first to request any variation, even if it was only holding off the mushrooms or asking for a sauce on the side. More recently, though, interest created by TV programmes and chefs' presentation skills has encouraged people to take greater control over their diets. As the hospitality industry reacts to changing dietary trends such as vegan or flexitarian dishes, restaurants need to up their game in providing for the discerning customer.

If you're not already familiar with customisation, in this chapter I'll show you what it means using examples of who's doing what and suggesting tips to inspire you to create a more bespoke and tailored experience for every customer. Showing that you're willing and able to meet a customer's dietary requirements is central to them enjoying their eating out experience. In prioritising their choices, you'll show them how much you value their custom.

Catering for vegans, vegetarians and people with allergies

Vegan diets have seen an incredible proliferation over the past few years. Whether it's simply cutting out meat and dairy for ethical reasons, or reverting to a raw food diet to support bodily health, veganism is one of the fastest-growing food trends in the world.

In the UK alone, the number of self-declared vegans increased by over 350% between 2008–2018, while one third of the population is consciously choosing to reduce their meat consumption. The best restaurants offer more than mere gestural attempts at vegan food, crafting carefully thought-out dishes, enhancing both their reputations and their returns.

Catering to vegans makes good business sense, and the more adaptable you are to change, the more successful you will be. The statistics, according to Mintel, show that the market for vegetarian food grew from £333million in 1996 to £786.5million by 2011. People who identify as 'flexitarians' are moving away from meat as their staple choice (which may account for the growth in the non-meat market), and this fact has caught the industry's attention. Research by Vegetarian Express in 2016 revealed that 74% of meat-eaters planned to try vegetarian meals out of home in the next year, while one third had already reduced their meat consumption, with 10% considering giving it up altogether.

According to research commissioned by The Vegan Society in 2017, at least 542,000 people class themselves as vegan. The report suggests the vegan movement is being driven by young people making 'more ethical and compassionate choices'. Supporting data from the NHS (National Health Service) suggests that approximately 2% of the UK population is vegetarian – roughly 1.2 million people. These are eye-watering statistics to contend with if you don't intend to move with the times. Therefore, it makes sense to embrace the shift in eating habits and offer your customers substantial and inspiring vegan options.

Without doubt, the hospitality industry has some catching up to do. There are some notable high-street exceptions such as PizzaExpress, which was an early adopter of veganism/gluten-free, including adapting its famous dough balls and offering plant-based pizza toppings. Wagamama also created an entire menu dedicated to its vegan guests that encompasses everything from Pad Thai to gluten-free sorbet.

Cooking to order and catering to dietary requirements isn't rocket science. In offering a couple of clearly identifiable vegan menu options, along with speciality non-dairy products that will complement a satisfying meal for your guests, you will attract the attention, and custom, of this rapidly growing market. Furthermore, the ingredients – vegetables, grains, pulses, etc – are relatively cheap to source as opposed to meat and fish.

The biggest investment you'll need to make is in your creativity so that your speciality dishes are as appealing to vegans as steaks are to carnivores. In delighting your new diners, not only will you open a new source of revenue, you'll also enhance your reputation.

It's vital, therefore, that your staff are as familiar with these dishes as they are with your signature ones, and they should convey the same passion and helpfulness in answering customer questions or making recommendations. The last thing you want is for a vegan customer to be left feeling as if they're the pariah of the party. If that happens, rest assured they'll waste no time in talking to social media about how your restaurant made them feel. Wouldn't you rather that social media trumpeted your restaurant as a hot spot for vegans?

One comment I hear time and time again from vegan and vegetarian friends is that they are tired of being offered unimaginative substitute meals when dining out. Meat substitutes (as meat-free 'mince', 'burgers' and 'steaks') have their place, but they belong more in the customers' store cupboards than on a meat-free menu. While the classic 'spicy bean burger' can be truly delicious, you can pick these up in any supermarket.

Meat-free diners would prefer to eat a meal that is premised around plant-based ingredients, rather than one where the meat has simply been taken out, which means you need to use the right food groups and flavours. Any other diner would expect no less. Also, don't forget that vegans feel hungry, too, and like to eat as heartily as the person on the next table. Attempting to satisfy their appetites with a salad or a stir fry is so last century.

There are many new vegan and vegetarian sensations to experiment with. Grains, beans, pulses, exotic toppings, seasoning, spices, fresh flavours, non-dairy cheeses and vegetables from all corners of the world open up possibilities to make vegans' hearts race with excitement, not sink with despair. These days, there are countless ways to cook without meat and dairy, and to do it with flair.

Food expert Amber Locke is a leading light in the exploration of meat-free dishes, and she experiments with vegetables as most chefs would with a joint of meat, cutting, preparing and cooking them in innovative ways to maximise their flavour and texture. She is also not afraid to try an increasing number of plant-based substitutes that replicate meat textures surprisingly well. Locke recognises that the modern vegan expects more from a restaurant than vegetable lasagne or squash-based risottos.

There's no such thing as an 'average vegan', so it's best not to second guess them as customers. Customisation applies just as much to your vegan diners and they increasingly expect representation and personalisation.

Tips on pleasing your vegan guests:

- Ingredient information should be visible and accessible using allergen icons on menus and information about dairy substitutes

- Include your vegan options with the main fare. If they're listed as alternatives, that's a sure-fire way to alienate your vegan diners

- Change your vegan dishes by seasonal produce availability just as you would your regular menu

- Be mindful of the principles influencing vegan choices – primarily ethics, health and environmental concerns – by choosing organic, local, and sustainably-sourced produce

- Personalisation is important and will allow those with flexitarian attitudes to choose exactly what they would like to eat

- Allow guests to customise every meal on the menu to be vegetarian, vegan or allergy free in order to keep everyone's options open. Statistics from Allergy UK suggest that food allergies are increasing among the population, currently affecting one million adults

- Educate your staff so they can answer guests' questions about the food from a safety perspective

- Collaborate with suppliers to learn about how the food is produced so that staff can answer questions

- Ensure proper sanitation and cleanliness to avoid cross-contamination in kitchen and prep areas

In 2016, the Labyrinth Holistic Café in Stockton on Tees won the Freeform Eating Out awards. It was praised for offering an extensive menu that included good-value, freshly prepared, attractively presented and 100% gluten-free dishes. It was also recognised for its strong community focus and knowledgeable, passionate and friendly staff who were completely allergy aware. Above all, the café was determined to deliver diners the best experience possible.

Cooking to order

Consumers increasingly want to know about not only food provenance, but also how it's prepared. Given the option, they relish the freedom to choose (to be in control of) how their food is cooked. Throughout my career, I've seen this trend explode. It's not uncommon to overhear diners requesting their aubergine to be cooked or prepared in a specific way, much like a steak. Me? I prefer mine chargrilled.

There's nothing more disappointing than ordering a succulent medium-rare steak and receiving a dry, overcooked chunk of meat – and this still happens. Offering the option of cook-to-order, restaurant owners must be prepared to get it right every time. It's a trend that rolls customisation and the clean-eating movement into one, giving health-conscious consumers a more personalised dining experience, making the meal feel more enticing. For the business owner, it's not a cheap option, and it may mean offering fewer dishes that can be cooked to order. However, this is offset by the fact restaurants can charge a higher price for these dishes, which fits with the habits of diners who are eating out less often but spending more when they do.

The DIY dining experience

On Zoë's birthday night out, she and Danny opt for a shared starter of prosciutto-wrapped scallops with lemon and parsley butter. The dish lives up to its subtly salted, smoky promise, and the fatty bacon protects the delicate scallops from drying out. Eagerly, they both pop a scallop into their mouths at the same time and savour the taste sensations, comparing their reactions in complete harmony with one another.

Not long after their plates have been cleared, Danny catches sight of their server heading for their table with polished ease through the busy restaurant. As the server places their steak tartare before them, Danny suddenly looks a little crestfallen. Concerned, the server asks if everything is OK with their order.

A little shamefacedly, Danny admits he's never eaten the dish before and hadn't realised that it would be served 'uncooked'. Without a flicker of criticism, the server offers a reassuring smile and says he is sure it won't be a problem to ask the chef to reinvent this traditional dish for Danny. With that, both dishes are returned to the chef, with the server informing Zoë she'll receive a fresh one as soon as Danny's is ready.

Laughing at Danny's embarrassment, Zoë tells him it's not a problem. Both agree that the server has been impeccably polite, going way above and beyond their experience last month in a local pizzeria.

The DIY trend is the ultimate when it comes to customisation. Many restaurants are giving up on endless lists of options and instead offering their customers a hot griddle and a choice of sides so they can cook their own meat. The customer gets their steak cooked exactly how they like it with their preferred seasoning, and nobody can complain to the chef!

Whether it is a humble salad bar or self-assembly desserts, the element of customer construction creates a sensation of DIY. However, this approach can have its pitfalls. It requires a lot of equipment (eg grills), results in more wastage than is necessary, and the guests will likely not be as good at cooking as your well-trained chef.

If DIY dining forms part of your strategic vision, consider deconstructing the offer with fewer choices available to the customer at each point. Or offer them a 'build your own' board, which works well from burritos to sundaes. As long as the offer is clear, the customer will feel involved in the creation of their meal and they'll have the control they hanker after.

Another way to look at deconstructing is to take all the elements in a dish or a drink and assemble them in an entirely new way. When a deconstructed cheesecake appeared on the UK television show *MasterChef*, it created a sensation and gave leverage to deconstructed menus. Similarly, the deconstructed latté, made famous by the tiny New York-based Coffee Project, encourages customers to experience espresso in its pure form, truly appreciating the constituent elements of the latté. Guests are instructed to drink from right to left, first trying the espresso, then the steamed milk, and finally the latté itself. Reaction to deconstructing coffee is mixed, while deconstructing cocktails has a bigger following.

Iconic themed menus

Themed menus can be a short cut into your guests' emotions. By picking a theme that you can perform to perfection, you will also reinforce your own brand identity.

While a venue looking to make a name as being quirky and cool might opt for *Alice in Wonderland* or a menu inspired by Haruki Murakami, those channelling class and elegance may choose *The Great Gatsby* or *Anna Karenina* as their muse. Tapping into a theme your guests will love shows you understand their psyche while allowing them to enter a world beyond the restaurant.

Picking a theme while retaining quality, aesthetics and class can be a difficult balancing act. Often establishments take it too far and the theme feels overworked. However, some venues are able to streamline and pare back the aesthetics, marrying both menu and décor to form a cohesive experience.

The Blind Pig cocktail bar in London's Soho has combined childhood classics with adult drinks. AA Milne's *Winnie the Pooh* is transformed into the 'Hunny Pot', while *Paddington Bear, Peter Pan, The BFG* and *James and The Giant Peach* are all featured with appropriate flavours and garnishes. What elevates the bar's Long and Short Great British Tales menu is the attention to detail. Not only does each cocktail look stunning, but The Blind Pig commissioned illustrator Masha Karpushina to tie together the drinks and stories with a menu designed to read like a children's book.

The Bletchley is the ultimate cocktail experience for any WW2 buff, or wannabe Sherlock Holmes. Staff speak as if they've been lifted directly from the 1940s and the war is still raging upstairs. Code cracking is intrinsic to the offering, beginning with the booking process and carrying on right through to ordering cocktails. It may not be the best place to relax with a quiet and well-crafted cocktail, but it's a must for an experience junkie.

Similarly, Scarfes Bar, a gentleman's club, displays the works of the renowned eponymous cartoonist on the walls. An illustrated cocktail menu includes original drawings and Gerald Scarfe's satirical comments.

Catering for the health-conscious diner

According to Mintel's 'Understanding Consumers' Perceptions to Sweetened New Products' report of 2016, a large proportion of people carry out their own research before making a decision to visit a bar or restaurant, especially as they regard dining and drinking out as a treat. Consumers have amassed a wide knowledge of healthy food and drinks, and they want to make more informed choices without feeling they are compromising on their sense of indulgence.

Every year, a new health and dieting trend is inevitably unleashed on the consumer. From the 1970s to the 1990s, war was declared on fatty foods, followed by salt, and then carbs. Today, sugar is the prime enemy. It's little wonder that restaurants and bars need to stay one step ahead to meet the latest demands.

Our diet should be well balanced, but food is meant to provide us with enjoyment as well as fuel. Life without a chocolate cake or a glass of wine isn't the life for me.

Sugar is correctly identified as a significant contributor to obesity when people overindulge (as are fat and carbs). But despite being labelled 'the new cocaine', it's not a poison, and it's naturally present in many foods, even items such as organic fruits, vegetables and grains. If we had absolutely no sugar in our diets, we'd simply become malnourished. Getting the balance right is the key, and the hospitality industry cannot fall behind in delivering the consumers' healthy preferences (including all ingredients, not just sugar).

To keep your menu fresh, relevant and profitable, you need to know how each item on it is performing and how it stacks up against your competition. Conduct an analysis of your menu every six to twelve months.

During this evaluation, look at profitability and competitive menu analysis to determine what works best and what isn't working at all. Then, make the appropriate adjustments.

Comparing your menu with your competitors' opens doors with regards to pricing, offering you a solid foundation on which to measure your profits. Performing a cross-sectional analysis helps uncover strengths and weaknesses in your plan, specifically in how your items are priced and presented. This way, you'll determine which items are popular, profitable, need extra emphasis, or need to be removed or replaced.

For the health-conscious customer, your business needs to consider the following:

- Customise or adapt dishes, eg swap white rice for brown rice or different grains or carbs

- Offer a meaningful number of dishes that highlight the 'naturalness' of the ingredients. 'Natural' is seen as synonymous with healthy

- Keep a large supply of fruit and vegetables that pack a punch, including wholesome 'superfoods' that deliver vitamins and nutrients

- Offer premium customised options that will keep guests on a health kick returning for more

- Create a drinks menu that contains healthy options that align with your brand and concept

Bespoke drinks

Friday couldn't come quickly enough for Shelly, a young and glamorous PA to the CEO of a large financial services firm, after a turbulent week on the Stock Market caused senior execs to lose their rag and pull her in different directions. As soon as she could, she picked up her bag and left the office to meet up with some girlfriends in a new cocktail bar that had recently opened in the city's vibrant heart. Shelly hadn't been there before and was keen to check it out and compare its margaritas with her favourites in the bar near the office.

Arriving first, she headed straight for the bar and found the last remaining stool. As she studied the menu, she caught the eye of the mixologist. He twinkled a welcoming smile as he prepared an exotic cocktail loaded with blackberry garnish, and they exchanged a few words.

Before she knew it, she'd told him all about her stressful week, and within a flash, he said, 'I've got just the thing for you. It's a gin-based pomegranate pick me up, good for stress, great fresh flavours. Would you like to try one?'

After he'd explained what the ingredients were and how he would make it, Shelly was captivated and ordered one straight away. She could always have a margarita when the girls arrived.

Traditionally, customers would have been impressed by a bartender recalling their 'usual' drink. More recently, though, customers are expecting a personalised cocktail experience.

Jerry Thomas, a New York bartender, is credited with inventing mixology in the 1860s, after his extravagant serving style turned visitors' heads at the bars he worked in. His signature cocktail, made of whiskey set alight and then passed back and forth between two glasses to create an arc of flame, was known as The Blue Blazer. Thomas initiating mixology as a craft – and a theatrical one at that – was certainly ahead of his time. He later penned the seminal *Bartender's Guide* which remains as fresh today as it was then. Thanks to him, mixology is firmly established as an art.

In essence, mixology has three components:

- The aesthetic
- The flavours
- The atmosphere

Today, more than ever, a great mixologist should be able to engage their customers, explain both their methods and ingredients, and be the centre of attention. Any talented contemporary mixologist will create beverages that look beautiful and taste delicious, all the while captivating guests with conversation and humour.

Sadly, though, not all cocktail menus come complete with a gifted mixologist to serve their bounty. There are few things more disappointing than visiting a high-end establishment only to have a cocktail served in a lazy half-pint glass, or the spirits added without measure to create an indistinct punch of misbalanced flavours.

Luckily, this is becoming a thing of the past as more mixologists become properly trained to deliver customisation and customer experience. And this training pays dividends. With the customer firmly at the centre of their focus, a great mixologist will ask them a series of questions about their preferences in order to create a perfect individual cocktail.

For example, the cocktails at London's Langham Hotel are described as 'emotional cocktails'. Bartenders tap into customers' personal experiences by creating drinks that capture their mood and essence in a glass. This often results in a combination previously unimaginable, thanks to the mixologists' renowned creativity and slightly eccentric ideas, but it is the essence of bespoke in a glass.

Taking this a stage further, some establishments create their own bespoke spirits. These can be sampled at The Connaught and The Athenaeum hotels, both of which have commissioned their own whisky. The East London Liquor Company specialises in homemade cocktails and will even bottle up a customer's favourite handcrafted spirit for them to take home.

Deconstructed cocktails are served in order for customers to gain a deeper appreciation for individual ingredients and their complex flavour profiles. Considering that spirits themselves feature countless carefully-crafted notes, it makes sense to pare a cocktail down, allowing guests to experience each element for its own merits before drinking them together in the cocktail. This can be a great experience for guests, but it does require the skill of an expert mixologist to get the right balance between sweetness, sourness and bitterness.

Health-conscious drinks

Following high-profile media campaigns, sugary drinks are very much *not* the flavour of the month. Consumers are increasingly looking to replace these with healthy yet tasty beverages, but it's not sweetness that they want to avoid. Whether they're fitness enthusiasts or hard-core clean eaters following a strict diet six days a week who allow themselves a 'cheat day', consumers on a health kick on Monday tend to be much more relaxed in their choices by Saturday. And this poses a challenge for the drinks (and foodservice) industry.

Consumers are no longer fooled by zero-calorie claims, and they're well aware of the health risks of sweeteners such as aspartame, preferring to choose sugar over such alternatives. Mintel's report 'Attitudes Towards Premium Soft Drinks' suggests that 25% of Millennials are willing to pay more for natural sweeteners, such as agave syrup. Mintel also reported that 62% of consumers will pay more for a premium soft drink with a clear difference in taste compared to cheaper brands. This indicates that 'taste should be a central tenet in brands marketing in this segment.'

Once again, the answer is customisation. Custom-made smoothies and 'mocktails' are promising developments in this area.

I've conducted my own research by approaching a number of leading bar professionals to obtain a better insight into how they are tailoring their offering, in particular to female customers. They have apparently seen a steady rise in demand for healthy items, loaded with fresh quality ingredients, premium botanicals and floral fragrances. These drinks are not 'boring' because they lack sugar. In fact, knowing what they're made of, where the ingredients are sourced and how they are served is a vital part of the customer experience. Think cold-pressed juices, shrubs, super-fruits, herbs and spices packed with live probiotics and endless health benefits, served in glamorous glassware with unusual garnishes.

Sugar is being reduced across the board, replaced by dried fruits, coconut or natural syrups to provide the sweet zing. 'Skinny' cocktails using fresh fruit such as watermelon or strawberries, topped up with coconut water rather than fruit juice, can still be indulgent.

This trend is rapidly attracting the attention of bars in the UK, and many are now offering their own distinctive creative flair, plus customisation that emphasises their individuality and sharpens their competitive edges. At Tredwells in London, the Gunpowder Gimlet is made with gin, cardamom, green tea and lime, and can be ordered without any sense of guilt whatsoever. The Grain Store, an industrial-chic restaurant with a vegetable-based menu, offers savoury cocktails, from Bloody Marys made with horseradish vodka, sours with aubergine rum, blood orange saffron Bellinis, to a sour cherry lemonade. These combinations show that it's possible to create the most amazing healthy drinks that see customers returning for more.

The element of customisation is key. Consumers appreciate the opportunity to add or subtract ingredients. Keeping a store of flexible flavours available, therefore, allows bars to offer guests a sense of luxury with a drink that's completely unique to the individual.

Following a strict diet can leave customers craving opportunities to enjoy the flavours they love the most. Women in particular are concerned about what they consume and are increasingly looking for 'authentic' drinks which are characterised by their heritage, or the craft that goes into them.

Bespoke soft drinks

Some of the most exciting innovations are to be found in the world of non-alcoholic drinks. Teetotal customers or the designated drivers on a night out no longer have to endure overly sweet, childish and synthetic flavours thanks to brands such as Seedlip, which has created 'the world's first distilled non-alcoholic drinks'. These drinks have been designed for discerning adult drinkers and contain aromatic blends of herbs, barks and peels. They can be enjoyed served with tonic and an appropriate garnish.

Leo Robitschek, bar director at the NoMad bar in New York, has a passion for creating mocktails for those who don't drink alcohol. In an interview published in Firstwefeast.com, he states:

> 'People see mocktails on our menu and wonder, "Are these for the kids?" No, they are pretty much for adults. The flavours are too complex – 99% of the time we sell them to adults.'

Other bartenders emphasise how non-drinkers don't want to miss out.

> 'This bar is about having fun. For us, it's about making sure that everyone has the ability to participate in that experience and feel that there's something on our menu for them.'
> —Erik Trickett, bar manager at Holiday Cocktail Lounge in the East Village, as reported by Forbes

Larger drinks companies, such as Fentimans, are also catering to the savvy consumer with their ever expanding Botanical Brewery range, which offers a variety of mixers and lower calorie premium drinks to appeal to many tastes. Fever Tree also recognised how a sourcing story can appeal. Launched in 2005, it has disrupted the traditional mixer market and has built its reputation for sourcing the highest quality ingredients, beginning with the specific quinine it uses from the Rwanda/Congo border. It has since expanded its range to include lemonade and ginger beer, always with the emphasis on quality botanicals and authentic flavours.

It's been evident that current solutions to the soft drinks industry's biggest problem – sugar – have been ineffective. According to industry reports, current soft drinks are perceived as 'boring', 'childish' and 'overly sweet'. Soft drinks lack experience, theatre and ritual that other beverage categories such as coffee, wine, cocktails or spirits offer in abundance. As an entrepreneur myself, I had to put my money where my mouth was and test the market myself. In fact, I decided to do it my way.

After years of studying the drink industry, hospitality trends and the power of customisation, I firmly believe that the soft drink industry got it wrong and completely misdiagnosed the problem of sugar in the first place. Hence all the artificially-sweetened solutions, tasteless water-diluted creations and the natural but weird-tasting drinks that are not performing well in the market. Consumers are unimpressed with the nanny-state approach of applying punitive taxes, constant criticising and patronising finger-wagging. Sugar in moderation is not the problem; I believe the problem is the lack of control over how much sugar each person wants in their drink to fit his/her individual lifestyle, occasion, taste preference or dietary requirements.

I set out to work on the world's first bottled drinks which can be sweetened to taste, driven by the belief that the future of soft drinks is bespoke, and we need to take customisation to another level. My vision was that the Kolibri brand would allow the customer to adapt and customise the sweetness and flavour of their drink according to preference, while bringing a new ritual and an element of theatre to the tired category.

Determined to listen to what the marketplace was telling me, I was meticulous with my research. My challenge was how to deliver a pre-bottled drink while offering a bespoke element. The innovation, when it emerged, was a lightbulb moment. The packaging includes a separate cap filled with agave which can be used to adjust sweetness and depth of flavour. Consumers are able to have their drink exactly how they like it, every time.

I didn't create Kolibri blindly; I was informed by consumer trends and the market in general. My belief is that bespoke is the future for restaurants and bars, but without having put my toe in the water myself, I'd lack credibility.

I won't pretend it is easy, but if you commit to integrating customisation into your own business, I believe you'll find new and wonderful ways of aligning your brand with your customers.

Tea and coffee

Even the humble cup of tea can be bespoke, and coffee, as we know from Starbucks, can be customised in many different ways, so it would be a mistake not to offer tea and coffee in a way that maximises their appeal.

Offering different blends and brands of tea and coffee, from the traditional through to the herbals, the decaffeinated to the most powerful, shows your customers that you take this important daily drink seriously. What's the point of going to the trouble of getting your food and drinks offering right if the tea or coffee you serve is a complete let-down?

Customers have hugely diverse expectations today, so stock a variety of milks, from soya and nut to plant. This will help satisfy many tastes, as will highlighting the provenance of the coffee beans or tea leaves you use. Modern customers are only too aware of plantation workers' exploitation and Fairtrade initiatives.

Beer

Craft beers are probably more popular than they've ever been, and consumers are becoming more sophisticated in how they pair the various flavours with the food they're eating. For example, the creamy risotto on your menu might be best paired with a crisp Pilsner or an American amber lager to balance the hops while staying light on the palate.

The website www.craftbeer.com has identified six of the main signifiers of a good pairing:

- Crisp and clean with grains
- Malty and sweet with beans and legumes
- Dark and roasty with grilled vegetables
- Hoppy and bitter with game and rice
- Fruity, spicy and sour with shellfish
- Tart and funky with rich meats

With all of these pairing ideas, though, you want your guests to enjoy experimenting and trying new combinations, so ensure that you and your staff are trained to give confident advice.

Soft drinks pairing

More and more restaurants are experimenting with soft drinks and tea pairing menus to appease alcohol-free diners and health fanatics. With the gradual realisation that an increasing percentage of the population is giving up on alcohol, the hospitality industry needs to meet a significant demand for alternative drinks that are exciting and appealing – and which will entice the customer to part with their money. The options exist already, for example Benjamin & Blum's sophisticated range of tea-based 'spirits' containing absolutely no alcohol, so it's up to restaurants and bars to stock innovative drinks.

The concept of pairing food with soft drinks was officially founded by René Redzepi at his restaurant Noma, in Denmark, where diners were served a careful blend of juice featuring flavours such as cucumber and whey, apple and pine shoot, sorrel, and nasturtium with his Michelin-starred tasting menu. In so doing, he created a trend that many wish to follow, given that alcohol consumption is falling.

However, it's not a matter of simply serving fruit juices as consumers are becoming more daring and their demands more exacting. They're seeking complex taste combinations with aromatic flavours, herbal infusions and fresh ingredients perfectly crafted to complement their dishes. They want to match intensity with strength, and they're not afraid to experiment.

Unlike with traditional wine pairing, the rule book has been thrown out of the window.

Premiumising the consumer's experience

For decades, wine has been presumed to be the beverage of choice for diners looking to complement their eating experience with perfectly suited notes and flavours. However, the world of food and drink matching has developed significantly, from local cafés to high-end restaurants. You could write a whole book (and many have) about the science and art involved in pairing wines with your menu. It's a subjective choice, though, and there's no 'right' answer.

However, here are a few general guidelines that should keep you on the right track when you're considering your recommendations for your guests.

Balance the 'weight' of the wine and food. A steak will be best balanced with a robust red, like a Cabernet Sauvignon or Barolo, whereas a delicate fish dish would be overwhelmed by this. Instead, fish should be paired with a refreshing but zesty white, such as Pinot Grigio or a light Soave.

Match ingredients. If you have 'fruity' ingredients in your dish, for example pork with apples, or duck with plum, think about wines with fruit undertones, eg Viognier or Gewürztraminer.

Consider contrast. The acidity in wine can contrast with the saltiness in some dishes. For example, champagne with smoked salmon or the sweetness of Sauterne with Roquefort cheese.

Versatility. If you are serving Asian foods with a lot of different components, you may need a wine which can complement the many flavours. A Sauvignon Blanc is a good choice with its cleansing acidity, or a Chianti that doesn't have too much tannin will be a good option to consider.

CHAPTER SEVEN

Eatertainment

'Eatertainment' is a concept that began in Dallas way back in 1982. When Dave & Buster's launched in a 40,000 square-foot warehouse space, it encouraged its diners to play games, from ping-pong to darts, billiards to bowls, and this was an immediate hit with customers. It was an exciting, fresh take on the eating out experience, and thus 'eatertainment' was born.

Eatertainment continues to prove popular with the brand, and as an idea it is now criss-crossing the USA, tying in to licensed movie promotions as well as offering eat and play combos. Customers can view the nutritional value of every dish on sale on Dave & Buster's website, from the ubiquitous wings to steaks, burgers and salads. If you have an allergy – yes, you guessed it – Dave & Buster's has an allergen-free menu, avoiding tree nuts, peanuts, fish, shellfish, soy, milk, wheat and gluten, so customers can order with confidence.

The success of Dave & Buster's has led to a whole range of competitive eatertainment offerings across the USA in particular, and it's a trend that is rapidly gaining leverage in the UK as a way of attracting custom.

Eatertainment is the dining experience that goes the extra mile in order to create a wow factor for guests, making their visit both memorable and shareworthy. In return, customers' Instagram posts and tweets form an important 'free' component of eatertainment venues' marketing activity.

Market trends in the UK are pointing to the fact that customers are eager for a more meaningful dining experience, and it's not just the Millennials clamouring for this; it is a trend that's capturing the attention of anyone who wants something they can't get when they eat at home with friends. Furthermore, they're willing to pay more per dish in return for eatertainment than they would for a standard restaurant menu. For a restaurateur or bar owner, eatertainment is a simpler, cleaner option than charging an entrance fee, allowing them to set their menu prices accordingly.

What the eatertainment comprises is basically down to the venue, its target demographic, brand values and how much it wants to spend. It can encompass a wide variety of aspects, from providing live music or comedy acts to a completely immersive theme which wraps around the entire guest experience. Naturally, your food and drink need to be outstanding, too, and remain a central talking point. A poor offering will simply nullify the entertainment experience, and the reverse is also true.

In this chapter, I'll be introducing you to a variety of eatertainment concepts that I hope will inspire you. In the crowded hospitality marketplace, eatertainment offers you the opportunity to refresh your venue with an exciting impetus that can reignite your existing customers' interest, while attracting new ones through your door. The ideas I'll present will range from the simple (but no less effective) to the luxurious and lavish.

Food as show business

'Molecular gastronomy' sounds as if it belongs more in a test tube than on a plate. I prefer to call it 'edible magic' as it combines science with artistry, and the results can seriously impress your clientele and satisfy their taste buds, while feeding their sense of adventure and exceeding their expectations. To me, these are all the essentials of magic; and the fact you can eat it is doubly pleasing.

Naturally, the first question that will spring to mind is whether your current food offering suits this transformation. My advice is not to let that deter you at the first hurdle, because as with any good magic trick, the secret ingredient is the element of surprise. In the case of food, this is the exploration of unexpected flavour combinations. You don't need to set your sights on acquiring high-end equipment because you can simply astonish your diners by presenting them with a dish they think will be sweet, when in fact it's savoury.

Playful interpretations of dishes are simple and effective ways to engage customers' attention and get them talking and sharing the dishes, thus elevating the dining experience as well as enriching the social occasion. Whether it makes sense for your restaurant to go to the next level depends on your vision for your brand and the amount of investment needed to acquire the specialist equipment and talent you'd require.

It takes not only a vivid imagination, but also expertise to produce mango spheres that look like fried eggs, cocktails that resemble marshmallows, egg and bacon ice cream or an edible Helium balloon. Some food innovations require low temperature cooking using a thermal immersion circulator or *sous vide* cooking. Other dishes require dehydrators to remove moisture from the ingredients, centrifuges to separate out liquids into component parts, or the mind-boggling trickery of an anti-griddle that flash or semi freezes foods placed on its metal top. It's food as physics – liquids to solids, solids to gases – creating theatrical puffs of smoke and vapours with incredible results for the diners' visual pleasure.

What interests me is the reason why chefs are creating these amazing dishes. The answer lies in presentation. The diner is invited to look, touch and taste the creations with surprise as the finale. By involving all the senses and evoking emotional responses, no matter how it's achieved, chefs create a more intense dining experience that adds to a venue's brand reputation for being unique.

Heston Blumenthal is perhaps the chef best known for pioneering molecular gastronomy. In many ways, he is to the restaurant industry what Alexander McQueen was to the fashion industry. Championing new styles that look amazing and cost the earth, Heston continues to amaze and enthral at his famous Fat Duck restaurant with dishes such as 'the sound of the sea', a complex creation that not only appeals to the senses of sight, smell and taste, but also hearing as the diner wears headphones while eating. The sensory experience is complete and they are transported to the beach.

Heston continually pushes the boundaries, proving that contemporary cuisine thrives on unexpected flavour combinations, challenging the eater with additional twists and playfulness, and he provides the pinnacle of the molecular gastronomy experience. His theories and practices are now being adopted by others who share his passion.

For example, Adam Melonas, chef at Dubai's Burj al-Arab hotel, created Octopops – orange flower-shaped lollipops created from octopus. Tom Sellers's restaurant, Story, offers edible candles made from beef dripping and Oreo-type biscuits made with squid ink and smoked eel mousse. Surprise unites them all as the key ingredient, proving that appearances can be deceptive.

The Alchemist in the City of London has elevated the drinks experience so that it aligns completely with its location, theme and design. Here customers are treated to an exotic range of bespoke concoctions, such as a hot-and-cold expresso mai which is served at two temperatures at the same time, or a vodka cocktail which has 'magic' as one of the ingredients. It certainly seems that way as you watch the colours change before your eyes.

Edible magic certainly creates illusions, but the result are real.

Creating an immersive experience

More than ever, guests want to participate actively in their dining experiences, and restaurateurs are finding new ways to immerse them fully with offerings beyond food and drinks. These range from simple one-off themed events to fully integrated design offerings with live performance elements. Eatertainment encompasses anything that will attract customers to a venue and engage them, and many venues have found its popularity regularly attracts repeat custom.

A restaurant could hold a poker night if evidence shows there is enough local community interest in the game. A bar could host a murder mystery event or hire a local band/musician. Eatertainment works on all levels, so it's no wonder it's becoming popular with brands.

'We are introducing more and more sophisticated live events at our restaurants, for example our music acts at Quaglino's, as we have found that they really entice new customers, and our regulars are happy too.'
—Jean-Baptiste Requien, D&D London

The examples I list below show the lengths to which some venues commit to serving their customers unforgettable moments beyond their food and drinks.

Bunga Bunga, Maggie's, Barts and Mr Fogg's are high-end eatertainment venues owned by the innovative and forward-looking Inception Group. Fogg's is based on Jules Verne's fictional character, Phileas Fogg, and actively invites the customer to immerse themselves into his world across four London-based venues, all of which capture Fogg's love of travel with interesting items from the places he visited. Customers can visit Fogg's Gin Parlour, House of Botanicals, Tavern and Residence. Each includes experiences ranging from gin tasting masterclasses to perfect afternoon tea.

The Gin Parlour recreates an exquisite Victorian environment, with upholstered *chaises longues,* gilded mirrors, ornaments and artefacts to invite curiosity and conversation. All the Fogg locations include Victorian décor and period-appropriate dress for the staff, which allows guests to feel that they've stepped back into a bygone age.

Far from resembling a museum collection, the brand has invested time, effort and research into creating unique experiences that excite all the senses. The drinks and cocktails are no less theatrical – who could resist a Tipsy Tea? Combine that with live entertainment, from magicians to jazz bands, and it's little wonder that Fogg's guests are keen to share their experiences on their social media and spread the buzz.

Alcotraz places the customer behind bars in London's first immersive prison-themed cocktail venue, where each drink is tailored to the customer, depending on their own choice. They then have to smuggle it past the prison guards. Upon arrival, guests don orange jumpsuits and are thrown into their cell, where the warders keep a watchful eye over them as they attempt to hide their contraband. If they're successful, they are taken to a bespoke cocktail bar where their illicit liquor is mixed into a tailored cocktail, without a menu in sight.

Dans le Noir creates an unforgettable experience by inviting guests to dine in complete darkness. On the surface, this may seem like a difficult experience to comprehend. However, it's designed to heighten the guests' senses with the intention of helping them experience their food in a different way – through smell, taste and touch, rather than sight. This not only offers diners an entirely different way to socialise with fellow guests, it also provokes reflection on how visually impaired people might experience dining out. Sharpening the senses in this way prompts the diner to think about what they are eating, and this experience is spreading to cities across Europe.

High-tech bespoke

New eatertainment offers and multisensory dining experiences are appearing each week. Venues are prepared to go to extraordinary efforts in creating immersive experiences to enhance guests' perception of the brand, which they then share with their friends.

Dinner Time Story began as a pop-up event using 3D technology in the form of an animated petit chef. Diners would follow the route of Marco Polo, roaming across a screen acting as the table top, and be treated to a visual feast as their dishes were digitally created right before their eyes. It has, however, become a phenomenal global success due to its unique appeal.

The six-course menu takes diners on an enchanting tour of the regions visited by the intrepid traveller while they share the tastes, sounds and scents of his voyage through delicious foods and carefully selected wines. It's a multisensory experience around a theme, accompanied by music, table patterns, props and decorations which all change according to the different chapters of the story, immersing the diner in a truly unique gastronomic experience.

The Chef Cam as seen at Inamo, a Pan-Asian fusion restaurant with a difference, is also gaining popularity. Inamo's stated mission is to 'strive to be renowned for our technology, and loved for our food and service', and the chain has excelled in carving out a niche offering where its interactive menu is projected on to the table surface, allowing diners to peruse it at their leisure and order their desired dishes using a cursor. The chosen selection then appears on the white plate in front of the diner.

For the more curious diner, the Chef Cam allows for a direct view into the kitchen so that they can stream the food as the chef prepares it in real time.

Music

Music is well-known for its subliminal effects, from the softer sounds that match a slower, more relaxed experience, encouraging diners to spend more time at the table (leading to increased customer spend on additional items, notably alcohol), to tracks with high-energy beats that encourage diners to eat more quickly. This is particularly useful for high-volume venues where the staff actively want fast customer turnover.

Many restaurants already showcase cabaret acts and live music performances as part of their eatertainment offering. However, some venues are discovering that in raising the bar, they are reaping rewards.

For example, Circus in London's Covent Garden never advertises what acts are appearing, so every night is a surprise. The acts can vary from aerialists to contortionists and acrobats, fire-breathers to hula-hoopers, burlesque and drag, all adding an extra drama to an evening out.

Bel Canto adds arias to opera lovers' aperitifs, while Park Chinois delves into the exotic world of burlesque in what it describes as celebrating 'the French love affair [with] the mystique of the Orient, resulting in a jaw-dropping interior and an unparalleled dining experience'. Quaglino's Q Aperitivo evenings are glamourous reflections of the sultry side of music with a live band at the bar, which is themed to match the cocktails and menu on offer at the time.

How you can adapt

Given the examples I've listed above, I understand that eatertainment may seem impossible to implement in your own establishment, taking into account venue size, location and budget. However, I want to inspire you. It's not impossible to create a bespoke experience for your customers that will set you apart.

There are many small ways you can implement changes that will have a significant impact on your guests. Music is an excellent start as it immediately adds ambience, and if you can include an element of live performance every now and then, your guests will be more likely to offer feedback. Adding entertainment to culinary delight is the best way to ensure that guests' experiences are truly memorable.

However, live acts only go so far in creating an extra special experience. Through introducing a little magic and theatre to dining rituals, you'll ensure your venue or brand will resonate even more with your guests. This can then be enhanced using direct interaction with chefs and staff, or customised mood-matching culinary experiences. Integrate these with your social media strategy, and you've nailed the new way of doing food business.

My top three eatertainment tips

1. Staff as storytellers. Educate and encourage your staff to share bite-sized stories of the chef's passion for his or her latest creations. Staff should completely understand the elaborate process that went into making the pastry the diner has just complimented, be aware of the provenance of the latest seasonal dish and know what lies behind the inspiration for each signature cocktail.

2. Let the chef meet the diners. Why would anyone want to imprison such creative geniuses behind a closed door? Chefs are a source of constant fascination to diners, who will marvel at their talents and their team's multitasking skills while they prepare the food.

Chefs who are encouraged to interact and engage will delight diners with tasting dishes they intend to feature on next season's menu, offering fascinating insights into the meal which will make any foodie's night out totally unforgettable. Allow your chef to share their passion and pride in the art of cooking. If nothing else, they can gather valuable feedback.

3. Encourage interaction. 'Open' kitchens, where diners can see their meal being prepared, are already a staple of casual chains such as Wagamama and PizzaExpress. Diners can even influence and customise what they will be served.

On another level, the 'chef's table' at high-end restaurants allows diners a close-up and personal cookery demonstration by a skilled chef. While this is an exclusive experience that doesn't come cheaply, any food service operator can learn from the consumer's desire for an intimate interaction, which be achieved in less expensive ways via one-off events such as cookery demonstrations, group classes and food festivals. These create further engagement with customers in a meaningful way.

What will make your venue the preferred choice in the face of growing competition? What creative choices are appropriate to your venue, your location, your food, and, of course, your intended customers? No matter how you enhance your offering through the introduction of eatertainment, though, remember the food must remain the centrepiece of your guests' experiences.

CHAPTER EIGHT

Bespoke Marketing And Digital Solutions

In Part One, we discussed how important it is to market your venue before the customers arrive for the first time, and how you need to continue their journey once they're inside. Just as importantly, following their visit, you'll want them to be posting their online reviews of the brilliant experience you created, along with their recommendations to their friends and families.

Even if you're not particularly media savvy yourself, you can be sure that many of your customers will be, especially the younger generations. The ability to harness the technology tools at your disposal will be an invaluable asset in connecting with customers beyond your premises.

When your doors are closed, the internet remains open, and customers may well still be talking about you. There is no such thing as dead time anymore, so the more you can do to make your story and offering available at all times, the better. Your customers are part of the ongoing conversations online, so these need to be part of your campaign. Whatever level you decide to invest in it, digital marketing is essential. It doesn't need to be expensive, just dedicate some time to it.

Social media and mobile technologies are playing an increasingly important role in attracting customers through your door as the more traditional methods are losing their traction. Where once printed vouchers in newspapers and magazines were popular, times have moved on. Customers prefer offers and incentives, delivered via their tablets or smartphones, that can be presented at a venue on screen for a seamless, convenient experience.

By involving customers at the centre of your story and offering bespoke experiences, you and your business will become personal to them, and you'll likely be rewarded with their custom. I don't pretend that this will be easy, because customers are critics too, and they're not afraid to share their opinions online. However, they can also offer you useful insights into what they would like to eat or drink, and their comments on anything from the décor to the bathrooms represent valuable feedback.

In this chapter, I'll offer you imaginative and creative insights into how to embrace the digital world in order to build on your customers' journeys, including examples where brands have excelled themselves in taking on the digital marketing challenge. Be part of the conversation with your customers – after all, as Oscar Wilde said, 'There is only one thing in life worse than being talked about, and that is not being talked about.'

Go social

As a restaurant or bar owner, you need to have social media at the top of your marketing priorities, and take it seriously. Social media is where you can talk to your regular customers and market yourself to new ones. It might be an activity you've neglected, or perhaps you've already made a start by creating a Facebook or Instagram page.

In this era of food porn, social media platforms are bursting with pictures of delicacies that influence customers, even the thriftiest, to spend extra pounds. If you want the orders rolling in, then it's in your interest to take advantage of social media to promote your restaurant online.

THE EXPERT'S OPINION
– MARK MCCULLOCH –

It is very important to bring value, entertainment, information and lateral content that is not about you, but is linked to you, when you're using social media. Your tone of voice is crucial; it's not about being salesy or pushy.

The brands that really get the power of social media 'let you in'. They talk about their brand story and people, their products and what makes them different. They create topical and relevant content, and if you can pull this off, you will profit from the incredible opportunities offered by the engagement of billions of active social media users.

Mark McCulloch, founder of WE ARE Spectacular

The question is, if you already have a presence on social media, are you really taking full advantage of the benefits it can deliver?

At a very basic level, social media is a platform where you can try out and tailor your offers through direct (and fun) engagement with customers using entertaining content, rewards and incentives. Half-hearted efforts won't do you any favours, though, so if you're not confident in managing your social media accounts yourself, recruit a local expert or a member of your team who can either teach you or manage it for you. It's worth doing and doing properly.

It's also a good idea to stay on top of it. Too many restaurant owners turn their social media over to whoever wants to manage it, often resulting in neglected pages, rushed posts, mediocre images and slow follower growth. Stay in control of the content and promotions, even if a third party is administering your account, and make sure that whatever your potential customers are clicking on is up-to-date and relevant.

If you're entering the digital world for the first time, with so many social media platforms to choose from, where do you start? My advice to restaurant and bar owners is that Instagram is king, Facebook is queen, and the rest are pawns. The key to going social and making a profit is to post top-notch food pictures and video clips. Refresh these on a regular basis, and don't allow your site/page to stagnate with offers that have expired. You'll need someone who understands the subtleties and mechanics of social media and has the time to do it properly, so it could be in your interest to hire a restaurant marketing agency.

Many restaurant owners are yet to embrace any form of online marketing at all. When TripAdvisor published its 'Restaurant Marketing Strategy' study in 2017, it revealed that over half of UK restaurant owners spend less than 10% of their time on marketing, and only 12%

have appointed a dedicated marketing person or agency. I found this to be a startling statistic, given that the survey was carried out by one of the world's largest online sites where customers generate content through their reviews platform. Of the restaurant owners that responded positively to the survey, a majority reported that their social media activity was their most effective marketing channel.

Even more surprising was the discovery that traditional print advertising didn't merit a mention in the top three effective marketing channels preferred by restaurant owners, yet most still spend more marketing money on print than social media. In my mind, there's a mismatch between spend and effectiveness which needs to be addressed and rebalanced. Clearly, the way forward is to devote funds to social media/online marketing, given its effectiveness over print.

The beauty of social media is that it offers your venue instant flexibility and measurability. Scheduling your posts at the right times to capture your target market's attention is one of its more brilliant tools. If you own a restaurant and want to attract customers towards the end of the week, then posting content on a Monday morning is probably not going to be as effective as doing so on a Thursday. Planning and scheduling your content, therefore, is crucial.

Some brands, both national and local, have seized the opportunity to cash in on the benefits of social media.

For example, Nando's, with over 4 million Facebook fans and 1.5 million Twitter followers, uses its fully integrated social media to engage with its customers actively on a regular basis, matching its fun content and promotions to its casual dining brand identity. By encouraging its customers to share 'finger selfies' on Twitter, Nando's generated an incentive tied into a gift card campaign that helped spread the word through customer-generated content.

Zizzi, on the other hand, carried out its own research in October 2016 and discovered that images of its food posted by customers on Instagram could have a major influence on diners' decisions whether to eat at its restaurant or not. The numbers were thought provoking: within the eighteen to thirty-five age bracket, 30% would avoid a restaurant if its Instagram presence was weak and the food images looked unappealing.

This poses a real dilemma for restaurants, especially when customers upload their own, often poor quality, images. Zizzi's inspired response was to launch a training programme for its staff so they could show customers how to take the best photo of the food on their plate – the composition, light, filters etc – so that it looked as good as it could when a happy diner uploaded their snap on to social media.

My top ten social media tips

1. Create ambassadors. Start social media sharing and turn your customers into brand ambassadors. Encourage them to share their experience with comments, photos and video on Instagram and other platforms.

2. #Hashtags. Have fun with tailored #hashtags which your customers can use to draw attention to their posts. Featuring these on your own platforms is a great fun way of involving customers in competitions or in-the-moment comedy.

3. Reward your online fans with exclusive offers, such as a digital coupon for a freebie dessert in return for talking about and sharing images of your brand on social media. According to Mintel, 74% of active coupon users responded by saying they would be tempted to try a new brand if they received a coupon or promotion code.

4. Storytelling. If you have an unusual or whacky way of preparing your food, or you want to introduce a new drink or dish that has a provenance of special interest, share its story with your customers. People love to feel involved, and stories help create more interest and loyalty in your brand.

5. Get to know your staff. Put the spotlight on your employees and place them at the centre of your brand.

This is a great way to celebrate your people's success stories with your customers, sharing their expertise. People like to connect with people, and this approach makes your brand feel personal.

6. Listen up! Social media isn't just about you promoting what you want your customers to hear; it's about you listening to them, too. Ask them to tell you what their favourite dish or drink is, and why. Invite them to post their own suggestions as to what they'd like to see featured on your next food and drinks menu, or create a fun online poll asking the questions you'd like to know the answers to.

7. Promote community activities. Share local events you think your customers will care about. Is there a great performance advertised in the venue next door? A charitable activity happening this month? Sharing an announcement from your restaurant not only helps promote these local events, it also gets your guests thinking about the occasion with your restaurant in mind.

8. Share good news. Every restaurant or bar owner loves a good review, and if there's one that is head and shoulders above the rest, either from a critic or a customer, share it and link back to the original review. Not only does it make you look good, it also makes the reviewer feel special. You could also offer the reviewer a free dessert or cocktail next time they drop by.

9. Follow trends. If there's a popular meme or hot topic suddenly trending that you can jump on the back of imaginatively, add the hashtag to your post, create your own spin, and get the world looking at your awesome food and drinks offering. Put your brand at the centre of the story, too.

10. Kitchen confidential. Offer customers a sneak peek into the inner-workings of your restaurant, such as a favourite staff tradition, or an image of you connecting with a local supplier. Any behind-the-scenes photos you post must paint a picture of how you do what you do without giving away your secrets, especially your recipes, to keep your mystery alive. It doesn't take long to write a kitchen confidential blog or shoot it as a vlog on your smartphone, and it creates content you can repurpose at a future date.

The importance of email marketing

Email marketing should be a key part of any restaurant's strategy. It's still the most resilient form of digital marketing, even though it attracted a poor reputation when spam became a big problem. When Facebook became the global force it is, email suffered another blow, but was thrown a lifeline when Facebook encouraged advertisers to boost their posts to a wider audience.

Email's effectiveness is only as good as your customer database, and with GDPR regulation in force since 2018, customers need to provide opt-in consent in order for you to market to them. Even if this means that you have to start again, email is still a tool to be reckoned with because of its ability to embed links, images, competitions, offers and news.

The trick is not to bombard customers with too many emails on a regular basis as this can prove to be unpopular. Used wisely with carefully tailored content, email should help you reward and inspire your loyal customers and showcase new additions to your menu and other exciting offers.

However, email marketing can be tricky if you don't execute it properly. If you're new to email marketing, it's worth consulting an expert to find the best strategy for your restaurant.

Bon app-etite

Ordering takeaway food online has been a firmly established practice for a few years, but with the rise of Deliveroo, Uber Eats and Just Eat, restaurants are tapping into the market where customers can enjoy their favourite food in the comfort of their own home.

App-based food delivery platforms are steadily on the increase, and more enter the market each year. Their presence is forcing restaurants to change their approach, particularly with regard to in-house ordering apps. These branded smartphone-ready programs are the perfect opportunity for guests to customise their orders, as well as access loyalty schemes and offers while sitting at the bar, waiting for pre-dinner drinks.

Technology such as this keeps the customer informed and able to monitor their wait times, especially in popular and busy restaurants. Apps also provide time-friendly ordering solutions, allowing guests to order food and drink from their tables, thus reducing waiting staff overheads, eliminating human error and cutting down waiting time. Brands such as Wetherspoon's have adopted this approach, and PizzaExpress's app offers exclusive discounts and allows customers to book a table or order takeaways.

More pragmatically, brands are developing apps that double up as payment portals. Once a customer has registered their payment information, they can then use the app to pay their bill. Surprisingly, the leading payment app across all trading sectors is one developed by Starbucks, which is now more popular than its nearest rival, Apple Pay. One of the biggest advantages of the Starbucks app, according to Harvard Business School, is that its generous in-built reward system links to its loyalty card with instant rewards added from the time of purchase. This immediately creates an uplift in sales. As of August 2017, rewards members represented approximately 18% of Starbucks's 75 million customers and drove 36% of its sales.

However, a word of caution. As the hospitality industry explores app technology, its overall effectiveness has yet to be analysed in detail, sector by sector. Early indications show that the popularity of delivery apps, coupled with the usual restaurant footfall, is seeing some kitchens struggling to cope. In response, some popular high-street chains are establishing 'ghost restaurants' built solely to fulfil delivery demands.

The patterns show that customers like using this technology, suggesting that in time many won't feel the need to leave the house at all if restaurant food can be delivered to their doors. As a restaurant owner, if you're incorporating apps as part of your customer experience, you'll need to think carefully about how you'll adapt and deal with these possibilities in the future.

On a more positive note, combining delivery apps with local pop-up kitchens will allow smaller brands to test the waters in reaching customers further afield. At the same time, it will give the app an element of exclusivity that will help draw customers and keep the cuisine on offer fresh.

Food bloggers and influencers

As a restaurant owner, you may find your biggest marketing assets are just around the corner. Leveraging your local network of food bloggers and those who influence local opinion can make all the difference to a venue.

Connecting with bloggers who then write about your venue is an easy, cheap and highly targeted tactic. There's usually a small price to pay in the form of free meals or invitations to special events, but in return, bloggers will help popularise your brand among their network. If you've not tried this approach before, I'd urge you to consider it, especially if you're located in an area with a high proportion of bars and restaurants where the competition is tough.

CASE STUDY – CIN CIN, BRIGHTON

Brighton, with a population of 279,000, is said to be home to 1,000 restaurants. Opening a new restaurant in the town can, therefore, be a tough call.

When Cin Cin planned on opening its second Brighton venue in 2018, it decided to hold an invite-only local blogger and press night. With over forty people turning up from print and online sources (social media and blogs), Cin Cin was rewarded with glowing reviews for its ambience, chef and food, accompanied by gloriously shot images of various dishes that feature on its menu.

Cin Cin Brighton has become a huge success, driven not just by the quality of its offering, but also by the evangelism of its customers online who are eager to spread its reputation. So much so, it was nominated as one of the city's Top 20 Restaurants (sponsored by a local business).

CASE STUDY – LEON AND THE BODY COACH

On a national level, restaurants looking to expand can tie in with celebrities in order to attract custom. Leon, a casual fast-food chain, has seen rapid growth since it was established in 2004. It has a distinctive vision – that fast food needn't make people fat.

With so many brands competing in the same sector, in 2015, Leon decided to engage the services of the Instagram and vlogger phenomenon Joe Wicks (aka the Body Coach), a health food guru to the stars known for his clean living. The chain's twelve-month campaign #LeanWithLeon created the perfect synergy between the brand and the influencer, with Leon producing a pair of branded fitness videos that it posted on both its own and Joe's platforms. In the first video, Leon's staff made up the onscreen 'extras', while for the second video, the brand recruited, via social media, extras from its customer base. Like Joe, they were rewarded with free emails and drinks in return for their services.

Who are the bloggers or the influencers in your area that are the perfect match to your brand? If you've not already contacted them, then perhaps now is a good time to seek them out.

Managing the digital universe

How often do you refresh your website?

What might have been an all singing, all dancing, bells and whistles affair two years ago can look stale if it's not been updated since. Most customers will view your web presence before deciding to visit you for the first time, so it's important you keep your site looking as fresh and contemporary as possible, with up-to-date menus, pricings and images at all times. A poor first impression can mean prospects will never set foot inside your venue.

Reputation is all or nothing in the digital age, and a restaurant or bar's online customer star ratings can either make or break it. Managing ratings and reviews and dealing with any negative responses are vital parts of your ongoing marketing efforts. Sometimes customers won't speak to you in person about something they disliked – or even liked – during their visit to your venue, but sit them in front of a screen with a wi-fi connection, and they'll bring all manner of things to public attention.

Below are some guidelines as you navigate the cyber world of the customer.

What are customers saying? The first step you need to take, even if your venue doesn't have its own web or social media presence, is to check out what others are saying about you online. From booking platforms and customer review sites to blogs, there will be opinions out there about your offering, even if you're currently unaware of them.

No matter whether you discover something positive or negative, treat all feedback as a valuable insight into the customer experience of your brand. The smallest of details can be reported – some of which might surprise you – and each needs your attention. If you spot a pattern emerging, such as comments about unhelpful staff or poor hygiene, then you definitely need to sit up and take action. Your customers will soon notice any positive changes you implement, and they'll be quick to point these out online to counter any negative feedback left by a previously unhappy customer.

Be positive! Nobody likes a bad review, but you'll solve nothing if you simply panic. Keep a cool head and read all the reviews, take in everything they say, and think carefully about how you'd like to respond.

When reviews appear on a website you're not currently registered with, sign up and create your venue's official profile so that you can engage publicly with your reviewers – both good and bad. Always be polite: thank reviewers and apologise, without grovelling, to people who post negative feedback. Where a poor review is justified, promise to make changes to improve the standard, thank the reviewer for bringing the problem to your attention, and invite them to return and enjoy the excellent hospitality you intended to deliver in the first place.

Ask reviewers you invite back to contact you directly via email so that you can offer them a gift (bottle of wine, free main course etc), but avoid posting these offers publicly otherwise you'll encourage a bandwagon of freeloaders. As long as you are genuine in your response (customers really don't like stock responses), your venue will be perceived as one that really cares about its customers' opinions. Remember, it's not just the unhappy reviewer you want to reach; it's potential customers searching through all the reviews, too.

Say thanks. Show your appreciation to customers who leave glowing reviews. It's nice to show your gratitude, after all, and these positive online interactions will help build your reputation further, as well as encouraging repeat business.

Invite responses. Never be afraid to ask your customers actively for online feedback. Reward them with an incentive – nothing too lavish, a free drink or discount on their next visit will do – and encourage them to be honest, be their reviews good or bad. Consider all feedback as an opportunity to improve.

If you're ever tempted to buy fake reviews from third parties, then don't. You have nothing to gain from these.

Wi-fi? Why not? Free internet access in bars and restaurants is almost a given these days. If you're not offering it already, then the likelihood is that customers will simply go and use your competition's hotspot. Customers are frequently tempted to 'check-in' on social media if they're using your wi-fi, which increases the chances of them leaving you an online review.

Bespoke marketing rewards through technology

The theme running throughout this book is bespoke. That is unquestionably the direction the hospitality industry is heading in, driven of course by changing customer habits, but also by the availability and application of new technology.

The ability to harness technology will play an increasingly important role in how we attract our future customers, allowing us to target them in ways that are unique and personal to them. Loyalty schemes are hugely popular and customers who sign up to them feel as if they are being treated individually. Naturally, developing or buying the software to deliver these programmes can be expensive, and currently, therefore, few chains are offering them. However, these will become the norm in the future.

When we see how technology can deliver customised data for each guest, tracking their purchasing choices, how much they spend, when and where they choose to eat and how often, it becomes clear that it will soon be providing us with the most accurate customer profiles ever. As it becomes increasingly acceptable for diners to use their smartphones in restaurants, digital marketing will soon be the centrepiece of the dining table.

Dining and digital

The restaurant industry – especially the fast-casual and casual sectors – has been experiencing a decline in custom since 2010. Research and statistics emphatically show that customer habits are changing, from how frequently they dine out, what they choose to eat and where, to how much they spend. We also know that customers are relying increasingly on digital marketing to influence their decisions on all of the above.

The common denominator that spans *all* sectors is that customers are making their decisions based on what feels personal to them. Restaurants and bars that provide tailored offers and experiences are steadily reshaping the hospitality industry, and I am of the firm belief that this trend will soon become the norm. If a restaurant or bar wants to thrive in this competitive marketplace, then bespoke is the way forward.

This conclusion is not based on my opinion alone, but on in-depth consumer research. Articles published by Accenture in 2017 show that 82% of consumers prefer brands offering tailored loyalty programmes that feel personal to them. One of the key drivers of this is consumer access to digital marketing.

For the hospitality industry, this presents a host of opportunities, as opposed to barriers. It may seem challenging, but it's possible to overcome these challenges even at the most basic level.

My advice is:

Talk to your customers. Influence their decisions before they step inside your venue. A conversational approach enables owners of bars and restaurants of all sizes and styles to build brand loyalty, create customers as brand ambassadors, and drive referrals, boosting both revenue and margins.

Reach out. The days of generic messages are over. Customers like to feel you are talking to them in a more personal way. Conversational marketing mixes traditional marketing, sales and customer services, making the customer feel involved in a one-to-one conversation that matches their interests, answers their questions and fulfils their needs.

Reach in. Technology allows brand owners to collect personal data from their customers legitimately. This data can then be repurposed in highly personal ways. For example, if you tailor unique offers for customers' birthdays, you'll show that you value them on a special and personal level.

Reach around. People love to give freebies or discounts to friends. Incentivising customers in the form of a special offer or a reward that they can then forward to their friends, you instantly create brand ambassadors working on your behalf who will help attract referred custom through your doors.

Keep talking, keep listening

Keeping the conversations alive once your customers have chosen your venue might seem daunting, given that you're collecting vast amounts of personal data on a daily basis. However, as technology advances show, it is possible to maintain it through the use of robotics.

That may sound counterintuitive and impersonal, but when you view it through the prism of the future customer profile (and customers' increasing affinity with technology), it is not so much science-fiction as science-fact. It won't be too long before customers are greeted by a humanoid robot, programmed with advanced AI (artificial intelligence) capabilities including emotional recognition and language processing to generate rich two-way conversations.

These robots will also become valuable tools in capturing important customer data. For example, is the visit for a special celebration, such as a birthday or anniversary? What is the customer's latest contact number and email address? This new breed of data capture (within the permissible regulatory guidelines) will encourage conversational marketing and enable brands to deliver highly targeted, personal offers and events to customers in the future, each with its own unique appeal.

My top three marketing tips

1. The online success of your restaurant is highly dependent on your offline performance, so it's vital to get your offline activities right

2. Provide and create online content that reflects your brand accurately, keeping it fresh and engaging

3. Don't do your internet marketing yourself. Engage a third-party expert if you want to stay at the top of your game. Work hand in hand with a professional marketing company to ensure successful restaurant marketing

A final note on effective restaurant marketing strategies

The marketing strategies I've outlined have hopefully inspired and encouraged you to take your hospitality business to the next level. I realise that marketing and PR is not everyone's forte, especially as it has varying levels and degrees of complexity. There are numerous professional agencies and experts that will help you, for a fee. If you do decide to engage a third party, it's worth searching online for 'hospitality PR agency UK' which will return a large number to choose from. You'll soon discover which ones will be best for you, and your budget.

No matter where you start, bear in mind all the points I've outlined in this chapter. This will, I believe, help you well on your way to taking the hospitality business by storm as you create bespoke experiences tailored to your customers. Remember, execution is everything.

Conclusion

The modern guest's 'no-one-is-quite-like-me' attitude means that, more and more, they'll visit your restaurant or bar with the intention of having it their way. In response, you must explore your guests' personal desires and reflect them in all your products and services, and across all touchpoints.

Hospitality guests expect their needs to be anticipated through orchestrated, meaningful interactions that create real value for them – not just marketing and sales opportunities for the brand. If their experiences aren't personalised and unique, the risk is that next time they will take their business elsewhere. Guests are notoriously fickle and, according to Deloitte, will these days spend less than a quarter of their eating out budget in their favourite restaurant. The rest is spent checking out new and more exciting options.

This book has been all about offering you the right ideas and tools to change, or adapt, your offering to suit the modern-day customers. If you implement and execute these ideas in the appropriate manner, you'll persuade your customers to remain loyal and return to your venue. Loyal customers are vital as repeat business accounts for at least one third of your revenue.

Incorporate options to customise food and drinks to reflect customers' taste preferences or dietary requirements into your offering. Stage unforgettable experiences that customers will share on social media and review channels. Pay close attention to your venue's interior design, including the restrooms – all are customer touchpoints that can create a good, or otherwise, impression.

Gone are the days of mass-produced media promotions. Tasty food, cheap drinks and comfortable beds are no longer the be all and end all when it comes to hospitality. Advertising and customer services require creative customisation that is tailored to a small audience of like-minded individuals.

There are six key points to remember:

1. Great customer service. In this 'age of the customer', ensure you train your waiting staff and greeters to provide a service that goes above and beyond. Unless you run a hot-dog stand in a busy airport, your business's survival depends on customers returning, and this is in the hands of your staff.

2. Attention to detail. The tiniest of details matters, from the creaminess of the butter, to how you serve the guests' coffee, or the quality of the ice in their cocktails. Even the provenance of the pepper in your peppermill is of interest to them.

If your food is served cold, customers won't return. If they have to wait too long for their meal – or, ironically, not long enough, depriving them of the experience of anticipation – they won't return.

3. Attention-grabbing menu. Make sure all your customer preferences and needs are covered, be they vegans or those with special dietary requirements, such as gluten-free or sugar-free. More importantly, allow guests the opportunity to alter your menu so it fits their taste perfectly. Your chef's ability to improvise with ingredients and understand all key diets is essential in meeting these needs.

4. Great ambience. Whether it's the lighting, the music playlist or the interior design, guests take a greater interest in places which add enhanced sensory value to their dining experience.

5. Positive word of mouth/reputation. Once people start saying that your place is *the* place, or raving about your food or service, customers will reward you through their loyalty.

6. Incentives. Give your guests every reason to return. Nurture your personalised relationships with them to encourage their loyalty and maintain these relationships by showing how much you appreciate their custom. Offer them exclusive perks, special offers or the royal treatment every time they visit. People love to feel recognised and valued.

I hope my experience and insights from the hospitality industry have given you a better understanding of your customers' evolving needs and habits. More than anything else, the modern customer values individual and bespoke experiences. You only need to make the smallest of adjustments to see how these experiences can change your customers' perceptions of your restaurant or bar. Even if you are working to a budget, you can still establish a truly unique and memorable venue which will set social media ablaze and have your customers returning, time and time again.

If this book has stimulated you to revitalise your venue and prompted you to ask the right questions, you'll be better informed to respond to the changing market and execute a tailored approach in developing your offering. Bespoke is definitely the way forward, and if you are as passionate about the hospitality industry as I am and want it to succeed, then I believe there are many more exciting discoveries ahead from which we will all benefit. Our high streets are slowly dying, so anything we can do together to keep them alive will be worth all the effort and passion we can muster.

Acknowledgements

I'd like to thank all those who have enriched and encouraged, inspired and enlightened, helped and supported me over the years, particularly in writing this book. Without your knowledge, insight, time, patience and generosity this would never have been possible. I'm particularly indebted, of course, to all those brands, friends, colleagues, experts and marketers who shared their experiences and donated their time in making this book as practical, illustrative and instructive as it hopefully turned out to be. Thank you to: Jean-Baptiste Requien (D&D London), Sam Bernard (D&D London), Martin Williams (M Restaurants), Andre Mannini (M Restaurants), Dan Munt (Gaucho Restaurants), Eddie Lim (Mango Tree, Chai Wu), Julio Marques (London Bridge Hotel), William Simmonds (Champneys Hotels & Spas), Jason Myers (Above & Beyond Hospitality), Kimberley Krebs (Hilton), Terence Sestili (St. Pancras Renaissance Hotel), Michael Tingsager (Hospitality Mavericks), Giuseppe Silvestroni (Harrods Restaurants), Simon Taylor (Condé Nast Restaurants), Tracey Howes and Fabio Adler (London Restaurant Network), Josh Craddock (The Doyle Collection), Abdul Yaseen (Michelin star chef), Simon Allison (Inception Group), Eddie Laposi (Restaurants at Google), Paul Matteucci (Vasco & Pierro's), Sabcho Gavrailov (Sopwell House Spa), Simon Stenning (MCA Insight), Liz Westcott (Mintel), Trish Caddy (Mintel), Nupur Saxena (Split Second), James Hacon (Think Hospitality), Mark McCulloch (We Are Spectacular), Charlie Cayton (Ferrero), Douglas Blyde (columnist and gastronomy advisor), Rebecca Hamblin (Kolibri Drinks) and Vincent Sitwell (Kolibri Drinks).

The Author

Kamila is a passionate advocate for the eating out market with in-depth industry knowledge. An insight and strategy expert turned food and drink specialist, she is dedicated to studying and sharing all developments shaping UK hospitality and foodservice through her blogs and other social media platforms, which attracted thousands of followers and positioned Kamila's brand at the top 1% of industry influencers.

Kamila moved from Poland in the mid-1990s to acquire her business education in the UK. She obtained a BA Hons from the University of Glamorgan, CIM and IBA qualifications and subsequently her MBA in Marketing. She held jobs that enabled her to work around her studies, managing various functions in bars, pubs and restaurants. This experience ignited something within her; Kamila's passion for the industry had begun. Unsurprisingly, her MBA thesis was on the subject of meeting guests' expectations in the foodservice industry.

Post-graduation, Kamila transitioned to working for global food and drink brands, always in marketing and category intelligence functions. There she was responsible for setting out of home strategies for leading brands, informed by data analysis and research. With a decade of hands-on experience in hospitality combined with her profound understanding of the market dynamics, and collaborating with influencers and insight experts, she took to writing about industry trends on her blogs.

Today, Kamila has thousands of followers with her widely popular blogs Bespoke.World and DivineEatingOut.com, where she has published over 300 articles, reports and white papers. As such she is recognised as the industry champion for truly bespoke and guest-centric experiences. Always keen to help developing talent in the industry, Kamila is also a mentor for women in hospitality and collaborates with key organisations championing women for board positions.

Recently, spotting a gap in the premium alcohol-free sector, and a massive industry challenge around sugar, Kamila set out to work on the world's first bottled drinks which can be sweetened to taste. She passionately believes that the future of soft drinks is bespoke.

Kamila can be contacted via:
www.bespoke.world
www.kolibridrinks.co.uk
www.linkedin.com/in/kamilasitwell

Printed in Great Britain
by Amazon